The Art and Making of

Blue Sky
STUDIOS

THE
PEANUTS®
MOVIE *by Schulz*

The Art and Making of

Blue Sky
STUDIOS

THE PEANUTS MOVIE
by Schulz

JERRY SCHMITZ

Forewords by **STEVE MARTINO** & **VANESSA MORRISON**

TITANBOOKS

CONTENTS

FOREWORD

By Steve Martino (Director)

Growing up in the Midwest, Charlie Brown's neighborhood felt like my own. Snoopy, Linus, Lucy, and the rest of the gang were like friends that I visited on a daily basis through the "Funny Pages." I was six years old when *A Charlie Brown Christmas* first aired and seven when *It's the Great Pumpkin, Charlie Brown* made its debut. These specials were family events and kicked off the two best times of the year for a kid like me. *Happiness is a Warm Puppy* was on our coffee table at home and I spent many hours reading and studying the drawings. Charlie Brown was the first character I ever tried to draw. So, when I started work on this film it was not lost on me that I was handling very precious memories. Friends and relatives would echo this sentiment when I first told them about *The Peanuts Movie*. The conversation would always start with great excitement to see these characters on the big screen again and end with some form of "Well, just don't screw it up!"

It felt like I was carrying Schroeder's piano, only it had grown to grand piano proportions and was heavy.

At the very start of our creative journey, Craig Schulz addressed everyone at Blue Sky Studios and told us that his father's friends and collaborators called him "Sparky." Craig wanted us to use "Sparky" when referring to his dad because he believed that he would have wanted it that way. It was an incredible expression of trust for all of us working on the film. The piano got a little lighter on that day.

Santa Rosa, California became a second home for us on the film because it's where Charles Schulz drew the strip for most of his career. Jeannie Schulz and the entire staff at the Charles M. Schulz Museum, along with Paige Braddock and the artists at Schulz Creative Associates, provided the invaluable connection to Charles M. "Sparky" Schulz and his original work. Every important story meeting with writer/producers Craig Schulz, Bryan Schulz and Cornelius Uliano took place in Sparky's office and was always followed by lunch at The Warm Puppy Café, inside the skating rink where Charles Schulz had lunch every day.

Sparky's drawing table, now located in the Schulz Museum, was my touchstone and where I found my deepest connection with the artist and his work. I would watch the video loop (over and over) of Sparky drawing Charlie Brown and listen to him sharing his thoughts about the strip. I was overwhelmed by the simplicity of the setting, from which he made such a powerful connection with millions of people around the world. Seeing the ink flow from his pen was like magic as Charlie Brown, full of expression, would appear on the page. It was here that I determined that our mission was to feel that "pen line" in every aspect of the imagery we would create for this movie. As he completed his drawing on the video clip, this quote really stuck with me:

> "WELL, IT'S A VERY GOOD FEELING TO KNOW THAT YOU ARE DRAWING SOMETHING THAT IS MAKING OTHER PEOPLE LAUGH."
> —**Charles M. Schulz**

I believe this was part of the motivation that brought Sparky back to his drawing table each day for fifty years and is what I love about the work we do in animation.

I felt that we had an opportunity on this film to present our story in a bigger way than ever before, while staying stylistically true to Peanuts. Sparky was a master of the comic strip format, and through his collaborations in animation with Bill Melendez and Lee Mendelson, he understood the opportunities that this broader canvas provided. Just as Bill Melendez took Snoopy to the air as the Flying Ace for the first time through animation, I wanted to take advantage of the artistic talent and technical capability at Blue Sky Studios to paint on the biggest canvas yet for a new generation of Peanuts fans.

When I read the comic strip or watched the TV specials growing up, I always wanted to look around the corner and see more of the neighborhood in which Charlie Brown lived. Our goal on this film was to take the audience into Charlie Brown's world and into Snoopy's incredible imagination and allow them to feel that these places really exist. I wanted to experience what it would look like if we were able to see those colorful Sunday comics through a sharper lens – one that allowed us to see the same characters, but with texture and lighting that reveals Snoopy's soft beagle fur and the cotton weave of Charlie Brown's iconic shirt.

I had the good fortune to work with an amazing group of artists who approached this film as "Peanuts fans" first and foremost and then brought their diverse talents to every aspect of the filmmaking process. Walking this tightrope of pleasing the fan in all of us and striving to create a bigger experience led us to feel like Charlie Brown at times. This quote from Sparky became a mantra that we all lived by as we faced each challenge along the way:

"I LIKE TO THINK THAT I COME UP WITH SOME SOLUTIONS NOW AND THEN. I SUPPOSE THAT ONE OF THE SOLUTIONS IS, AS CHARLIE BROWN, JUST TO KEEP ON TRYING. HE NEVER GIVES UP. AND IF ANYBODY SHOULD GIVE UP, HE SHOULD."
—Charles M. Schulz

The great thing about the team on this film is that they never gave up. The artwork and stories contained in this book provide a glimpse of our journey and showcase the creativity of these incredible artists. This is the work of my friends, who partnered to protect our precious memories of Peanuts and will hopefully create some new ones. Together they made the weight of that once-heavy piano feel more like a toy.

Opposite and Below: *By Steve Martino*

FOREWORD

By Vanessa Morrison (President, Twentieth Century Fox Animation)

Above: Franklin's first appearance in Peanuts, July 31, 1968

I was first introduced to Peanuts by my father as a child. He was a physicist by profession, but a humorist at heart. He loved not only the sly wit of Charles Schulz, but the simple, profound truths of Peanuts. My father was not a huge consumer of fiction, preferring his science books, but he loved poetry, and Peanuts was poetry. We relished the Sunday strips and it was always a special occasion when he read them out loud, most times punctuated by a big, knowing laugh – like a joke shared between friends.

My mother, too, was a Peanuts connoisseur. As a school teacher in the sixties she appreciated the quiet, knowing way Peanuts so gently nestled into the times. As an African American family we not only loved Charlie Brown and Snoopy, but also took great pride and ownership in Franklin, one of the few African-American comic strip characters of the time. He looked like us, had a quiet intelligence, and was cool!

Though we never met him, we also felt a pride and personal investment in Charles Schulz, the man. Growing up in Northern California, I knew that he loved his humble town of Santa Rosa. Every Christmas we heard tell on the news of all the great ice skaters that would come to Santa Rosa to the ice rink he treasured.

I made my first trip to Santa Rosa as an adult in the fall of 2011. The amazing Jean Schulz and indefatigable Karen Johnson gave me a very special, moving tour of the Charles M. Schulz Museum. It is a national treasure. To see the office where Charles Schulz created his timeless strips, to see the table where he had lunch every day in The Warm Puppy while watching the local kids skate, and then to cross the street to the galleries and see the immense body of work that has touched people around the world for generations was awe-inspiring. It is a magnificent, special soul who can inspire and summon such profound universal truths about humanity from the perch of his front porch.

Bringing Peanuts to the big screen has been an enormous effort. Everyone involved has felt a great sense of pride, honor, and duty associated with translating Schulz's vision into a feature-length CG movie. Craig Schulz and Bryan Schulz took painstaking care to make sure that the story paid tribute to Schulz's work and, along with collaborator Cornelius Uliano, honored their father and grandfather and the legacy. Our fearless director Steve Martino came to Peanuts with a passion for the artistry of Schulz's "line" and storytelling, but also brought a unique vision for how to thoughtfully and intelligently craft a new artistic interpretation of Peanuts rooted in all that we know and love. Producer Paul Feig brought insight into the movie that was informed by his deep and lifelong personal connection to the trials and tribulations of Charlie Brown and the gang. Fox Animation's Ralph Millero was the super-fan who lived and breathed Peanuts with a fervor that kept everyone on track.

And then there were the spectacular artists and production wizards at Blue Sky. Every single artist at Blue Sky came to *The Peanuts Movie* with a deeply personal appreciation for the importance of Peanuts and Schulz. Brian Keane, Paul Ohrt, and producer Mike Travers helped create a truly special production environment that marshalled and supported the artists' efforts. The devotion with which the entire studio approached staying true to Peanuts and the insightful way they let it breathe and evolve was amazing to watch. I think that all of Blue Sky would echo my feeling that this has been a journey of a lifetime.

I give profound thanks to the good people at Peanuts Worldwide Entertainment, Creative Associates, and the Schulz family for bringing us into the fold. We are humbled and deeply grateful to have been able to be a part of Sparky's world.

Above: Peanuts, January 27, 1980

Below: Snoopy cracking the whip with Linus's blanket at the pond -
Design by Jon Townley, Color by Vincent Nguyen, Poses by BJ Crawford

LEGACY
It's Hard to Believe You're 65, Charlie Brown!

Above: The first Peanuts strip, featuring Shermy, Patty and "Good ol' Charlie Brown," October 2, 1950

"THE ONLY THING I EVER WANTED TO BE WAS A CARTOONIST. THAT'S MY LIFE. DRAWING."
— Charles M. Schulz

"I always thought of my dad as the great observer," reminisces Craig Schulz. "No matter where he was or what he was doing, he would find a comic strip in the moment. Whether it was a tennis match, a game of golf or just ordinary life, he never missed an opportunity to tell a story."

On October 2, 1950, Charles M. Schulz began a fifty-year journey of sharing those observations with the world. Through a comic strip that made its debut in just seven newspapers across the country, he introduced readers to the characters of Shermy, Patty and Good ol' Charlie Brown. Over the years, Schulz would introduce the rest of the characters that are now staples in pop culture.

By the end of the 1960s, Peanuts had reached millions more fans through publishing, licensing and marketing partnerships. Although the first licensed Peanuts products were paperback books published in 1951, it was a 1960 comic strip featuring the now-iconic motto "Happiness is a Warm Puppy" that launched the characters into the stratosphere of the licensing industry. The "Happiness is..." phrase had caught the attention of Connie Boucher, founder of Determined Productions, who approached Schulz with the idea of publishing a book based around it. Schulz was at first reluctant, but agreed, penning additional "Happiness is..." sayings. The book spent forty-five weeks on the New York Times Best Sellers list... An industry was born.

Today, the Peanuts characters are an ongoing merchandising and marketing force with long-standing relationships with top brands still in place. For example, 2015 marks the fifty-fifth anniversary of the brand's relationship with Hallmark, the characters have been featured in the Macy's Thanksgiving Day Parade since 1968 and MetLife celebrates thirty years with Snoopy and the gang as spokes-characters. The Schulz family has stayed involved with the creative direction and positioning of all things Peanuts related, still working out of offices in Santa Rosa, California, where Charles Schulz's art studio was located.

Yet through all the books, apparel and toys, it was always all about story and character for Charles M. Schulz. With a knack for social commentary, Schulz would

Top: Lucy coins the now-iconic phrase in Peanuts, April 25, 1960
Above: Snoopy's alter-ego Joe Cool makes his first appearance, May 27, 1971

"*The beauty and perfection of Charles Schulz was how he captured children and the way they think, and I love how he captured their perception of adults. I also love that he could be sardonic but never mean. Playing Sally in* You're a Good Man, Charlie Brown *on Broadway was one of the best memories of my career.*"

— **Kristin Chenoweth,** actress

introduce characters and storylines with wit, sarcasm, humor and heart. In the mid-1960s, he introduced the character Peppermint Patty. A tomboy at heart, she excelled in sports and served as the manager of a rival baseball team. While that may seem benign to most now, the introduction of girls playing sports on the same team as boys was nearly a decade ahead of its time. By today's standards, it is incomprehensible to think of a character's introduction to a comic strip as "controversial," yet that is exactly what occurred in 1968 when Schulz introduced Franklin to the cast, the first African-American character featured in the strip. Encouraged by schoolteacher Harriet Glickman, Schulz introduced the character of Franklin on a beach to a vacationing Charlie Brown and later incorporated him into the strip as a classmate of Peppermint Patty and Marcie. Schulz received letters of opposition, which he ignored. Schulz was able to further expand his voice through the various personas of his alter-ego Snoopy, most notably Joe Cool, the World Famous Author and of course, the World War I Flying Ace.

Schulz possessed the natural ability to organically and seamlessly weave relevant

Above: Snoopy's doghouse burns down, but Charlie Brown saves the day in Peanuts, September 19, 1966, September 20, 1966, and October 4, 1966

topics into the panels of his strips as if they were self-evident. "Through it all, my dad never took advantage of his position," says Craig Schulz. "In fifty years, he never turned cynical about the world around him and that paid off. People genuinely care about these characters. I remember when Snoopy's doghouse burned down," he adds. "People sent him money to help rebuild it!"

Bordering the top of a wall in the main conference room at Charles M. Schulz Creative Associates at One Snoopy Place in Santa Rosa is a line-up of each of the major Peanuts characters: Shermy, Patty, Pigpen, Violet, Sally, Schroeder, Linus, Charlie Brown, Snoopy, Lucy, Woodstock, Peppermint Patty, Marcie, Franklin, Rerun and Frieda. When seated at the table, it gives the impression that the characters are watching over all the activity in the room.

"We always say that each of the characters represents a piece of our dad," says Craig Schulz. "Charlie Brown was his real self, while Snoopy is what he wanted to be. The reality is that each of us can find an identifiable character to relate to."

The universal appeal of the characters, whether it is the crabbiness of Lucy, the heart of Linus, the introspection of Marcie, or one of the many personas of Snoopy, is without question why the strip and its characters have remained relevant as Peanuts nears its sixty-fifth anniversary.

By the time the strip completed its run in 2000, Peanuts had an estimated readership of over 350 million people, in 2,600 newspapers, representing twenty-one countries around the world. With a combined grand total of 17,897 strips (15,391 daily; 2,506 Sunday), each one drawn, inked and lettered by Schulz, the comic continues in syndication, reaching new readers every day.

The list of accomplishments and accolades bestowed upon Peanuts is, in a word, impressive: fifty primetime network TV specials, four Emmy awards, an additional thirty-two nominations, four Peabody awards, two Grammy awards, four feature animated films, an Oscar nomination, a Broadway musical, two Tony awards and multiple magazine covers on *Time*, *Newsweek*, *LIFE*, *Rolling Stone*, *TV Guide* and *People* (to name a few). To say the strip and its characters have made an indelible impact from the mid-twentieth century to the present would be an understatement.

This year, that legacy continues with the return of the Peanuts gang to the big screen after a thirty-five-year absence, and for the first time ever in CG.

Above: Charles Schulz announces his retirement in the last Peanuts strip, February 13, 2000

This spread: Charlie Brown and the Peanuts gang at the fence trying to see the new neighbor -
Design by Tyler Carter, Color by Robert MacKenzie

NEW ADVENTURE
You're Going Back to the Big Screen, Charlie Brown!

It has been thirty-five years since the Peanuts gang appeared on the big screen. Over the decades, the Schulz family held fast in resisting suitors knocking on their doors with screenplays, pitches and "fresh takes" on Charlie Brown and Snoopy.

But about eight years ago, the Schulz family received a call from Blue Sky Studios. "They asked, just as everyone else had asked, if we would be interested in doing a movie," recalls writer/producer Craig Schulz, who replied with a courteous, "Thanks, but no thanks."

"But then they asked if they could just show us some material. I replied, 'Sure, but we'll never do a movie.'"

Never say never.

Enter director Steve Martino, who very passionately made a case for Blue Sky's vision to bring the beloved characters back to the big screen. While at first very skeptical, there was something about the look of early concept work the artists at Blue Sky created that caught Craig Schulz's attention, not to mention his imagination. "When you *looked* at the world – the trees, the ice, the snow – I knew then that if you could do it right, it would be spectacular."

For the next few years, Twentieth Century Fox Animation executive Ralph Millero diligently and passionately nurtured the relationship with Craig Schulz, Jean Schulz and the family. Finally, in 2012, Craig Schulz phoned up Millero and said, "We have a story and script." Millero took the script to Twentieth Century Fox Animation President Vanessa Morrison, who immediately set the wheels in motion. Fox and Blue Sky had done what every studio had attempted: secured the rights to one of the world's most sought-after groups of characters.

It is one thing to assign a license's rights to a producer or a studio, but when those rights involve a sixty-five-year-old beloved global iconic property whose characters have resonated with fans spanning multiple generations, the task is one that cannot be treated lightly.

"We were very lucky to get Steve Martino on board," says Craig Schulz. "Over the years, we had dealt with a lot of people who would come in and say they've grown up with Peanuts, that they had a great story, but the reality is that it is not that easy to step into the world my dad created, to understand how he drew the strip. Steve Martino got it."

For Martino, the feeling was more than mutual. "It was a humbling moment," recalls the director. "I think a big part of the connection that we had is that Craig [Schulz] looked at the work we had done on past films, like the way we handled the Horton film [*Horton Hears a Who!*], staying true to the style of Dr. Seuss."

"I almost fainted when Ralph [Millero] approached me to work on the film," jokes producer and life-long Peanuts fan Paul Feig. "It was like getting the phone call to come on board for the remake of *Star Wars*."

When Martino received the official news that he and his team at Blue Sky Studios had been given the green-light to move forward with a feature adaptation of Peanuts, to say that the director felt a little bit of pressure would be an understatement. "I thought about Schroeder and his little toy piano, and on the day we were entrusted with these icons, I felt like I had a grand piano on my shoulders. I had artists lining up outside my door!"

Supervising animator Nick Bruno had a similar experience. "It was the first time my dad called with an opinion on how not to screw up a project of ours!" he recalls.

Martino also recounts a conversation he had with writer/producer Craig Schulz during an early meeting on the project: "Charles Schulz had a profound impact on me as a child and as an artist," says Martino, "and in one of our initial meetings, Craig stopped me and said, 'All of my dad's friends referred to him as Sparky, so if we're going to be on this journey together, that is what you should call him.' That was such a great honor that he would say that to me."

To kick off production, Craig Schulz brought acclaimed artist Tom Everhart to Blue Sky Studios to meet with the filmmakers. With a relationship that dates back to 1980, and as the only artist educated, trained and authorized by Charles Schulz to reproduce the characters in the medium of fine art, Craig Schulz thought Everhart would be able to share his perspective on translating the characters to a new medium with the production team. Everhart's larger-than-life interpretations of Snoopy, Charlie Brown and the gang have appeared in numerous galleries all over the world, including the Louvre Museum in Paris, the Los Angeles County Museum of Art, the Suntory Museum of Art, Tokyo, Japan, and of course, the Charles M. Schulz Museum in Santa Rosa, California.

"He came here with loads of enthusiasm," recalls Martino. "We all care about these characters and felt a responsibility to carry that forward and it was clear to us that Tom shared that passion."

Martino still recalls Everhart recounting the advice Schulz gave to the painter as Everhart related the story of how he met the legendary cartoonist. "Sparky encouraged Tom to 'explore the canvas you're painting on.' And to see how Tom translated the characters of the comic strip to works of art was eye-opening."

To illustrate how he analyzed the work of Schulz, Everhart projected images of the cartoon strip on a movie screen, demonstrating how the painterly ink lines translated to his broad painterly brush strokes that grace the canvas of his paintings.

"When Tom blew up the strip, we saw such detail in the line and literally saw *story in the line*. It was incredible," says Martino. "It really was a paradigm shift for us," adds art director Nash Dunnigan. "We knew then we had our launching pad for the look and style of the characters and production design."

This spread: Charlie Brown and Snoopy walking in their backyard - *Final Digital Art*

ROAD TRIP, SNOOPY!
(The First of Many, Many, MANY Road Trips)

Admit it. At one point in your life, an attempt was made to doodle a version of Snoopy or his doghouse on a school notebook or scribble the iconic zigzag of Charlie Brown's sweater. Or perhaps you traced the characters from the Sunday comics. "When I was younger, I thought, 'I can draw Charlie Brown, it's simple,'" recalls Martino. "But when you really look closely at what [Schulz] had done and try to replicate that, it's daunting!"

Needless to say, the Blue Sky crew immersed themselves in the world of Peanuts. What better way to start than at the Charles M. Schulz Museum and Research Center in Santa Rosa, California?

Although the museum doors did not open until August 2002, after his passing (in February 2000), Charles Schulz was involved with each and every design stage, as was his wife, Jean Schulz, who now serves as the museum's board president. Boasting a comprehensive research center dedicated to Schulz's work and legacy, the museum also houses a vast collection, including thousands of sketches, pieces of artwork and comic strips featuring the Peanuts characters, as well as earlier works and personal memorabilia.

"The folks at the Schulz Museum were phenomenal," says Martino. "They opened up their archives to us and were extremely welcoming of us just being there and exploring."

And explore they did.

On the second floor of the museum is Schulz's drafting table and office, recreated just as he left it. It was there where Martino truly felt connected to his childhood idol. "When I walked into that space, I saw connections to who I am. Yes, he was an artist, but he also loved sports. He played golf. I played golf at Alter High School [Dayton, Ohio] – still do – and played some soccer, hockey, and all of these cues were on the walls. I felt a connection to things he was passionate about," says Martino. "To be surrounded by his books and all the things in his office as we set out to work was both humbling and inspiring."

The team delved right in and started to absorb the surroundings and the world of Peanuts. "We wanted to learn everything about Sparky's life, how he approached his work sitting right over there at that desk," recalls Martino. "I dearly would have loved to have met him."

The crew held all their meetings in a conference room just outside Sparky's office. Adorning the walls were framed pictures of all the iconic characters from the strip, which served as inspiration for the crew in developing the various story arcs throughout the film.

The story team, led by head of story Jim Kammerud and story artist Karen Disher, were part of the initial group that traveled to Santa Rosa for what would become the first of many, many, *many* expeditions. "I think I travelled to Santa Rosa on average about one week out of every month over the past few years," states Kammerud.

In this age of computer-generated imagery, most storyboard artists have migrated from pencil and paper to working digitally. "We used to storyboard everything on paper, but now we storyboard on tablets, so you're basically drawing on a TV screen, which is great, because there's an 'undo' button," explains Kammerud. "But when we would go to Santa Rosa and sit around the conference room near Sparky's office, all of a sudden we're working with pencils and pads of paper in this room full of Sparky drawings, put on the spot to draw, and there's no 'undo' button!"

"And not only are you surrounded by his drawings, his heirs are sitting across the table from you," adds Disher, jokingly. "So you've got Schulzs *looking* at you, watching, and you're trying to not butcher their dad and granddad's characters. It definitely took a couple visits to Santa Rosa before I could comfortably draw in front of them, but in the end, it is just like learning to draw any new character; it takes a while to get up to speed." Staying on model for thousands of storyboards would prove daunting to the most seasoned of artists, and confesses Disher, "I never quite figured out how to make Linus look absolutely right without literally tracing over the comic strip!"

To gain insight into the subtleties of Schulz's talent, the artist, animators and story team turned to Charles M. Schulz Creative Associates' Paige Braddock. As Creative Director, a post she has held since 1999, Braddock leads a team of seventeen and is responsible not only for the look and creative development of all Peanuts-related product produced worldwide, but all editorial direction of publishing initiatives as well. She is also the creator of the widely read comic *Jane's World*, which received a 2006 Eisner nomination for best humor book.

"Paige was an invaluable resource to all of us," states Martino. "She really was the last artist to work and train with Sparky."

Martino invited Braddock to Blue Sky Studios to meet with the crew so they could all hear firsthand about the approach to the strip and drawing style of Schulz from someone who had actually worked with the cartoonist. Braddock's advice could be

Above: Early Charlie Brown ink sketchbook drawing - *Sketch by Steve Martino*
Right: Early Woodstock ink sketchbook drawing - *Sketch by Steve Martino*

"The process, working with the Schulzs and getting a story that felt both true to the property and not a retread or something you've seen before but rather a story that could have been told by Sparky, this really is an extension of his legacy."

— **Michael Travers**, Producer

"At first I thought, 'This is going to be so easy, it's just smiley faces. Charlie Brown is just a smiley face, right?' It is amazing how hard it is to get a simple circle and a smile to look like Charlie Brown."

— **Jim Kammerud**, Head of Story

Below: Animation sketch pose planning: Snoopy primes the snowball for Charlie Brown to pitch - *Thumbnails by Garrett Shikuma*

Above: Animation sketch pose planning, animation blocking and final render - *Animation by Garrett Shikuma*

summed up in one word: Relax. "Schulz's line was loose and organic. You can't even get close to that line quality if you can't relax yourself," says Braddock.

She also reassured the artists they were not alone in feeling a bit overwhelmed by recalling her early challenges in mastering the characters. "Definitely Charlie Brown's head," says Braddock, referring to the hardest character trait to ink. "It is nearly impossible to get right when you first start working with the characters, and if it is off in the least, it really stands out."

The crew really knew they had their work cut out for them and would need to push the envelope once they were given the screenplay by Craig Schulz and writing partners Bryan Schulz and Cornelius Uliano.

The idea for the story actually came to Craig Schulz during the Christmas holiday season while visiting a nearby mall. "Our local radio DJ sponsors a Secret Santa program for charity," recalls Schulz. "You donate money and then he would play a dedication song, so I asked him to play the song 'Snoopy's Christmas' by The Royal Guardsmen." An American rock band from the 1960s, The Royal Guardsmen are best-known for their 1966 Gold Record song 'Snoopy vs. the Red Baron.' Released in 1967, 'Snoopy's Christmas' was a follow-up song to that smash hit. "As I listened to the song I could literally visualize the look to the story and I thought that it might actually make a great film."

Schulz knew they would need to expand the conflict between Snoopy and the Red Baron and then weave that story into the film's main narrative of Charlie Brown's story arc. Together with Bryan Schulz's writing partner Cornelius Uliano, the three hammered out the screenplay that was ultimately optioned by Twentieth Century Fox Animation's Vanessa Morrison and the rest is history.

"It's been eight years, but I think working with Steve and everyone at Blue Sky, we've really stayed true to the vision of our original draft," says Craig Schulz.

Originally, the writers thought about focusing the story more on Snoopy, with Charlie Brown relegated to a secondary plot, but they quickly decided against that direction, knowing that too much Snoopy could potentially overpower the film's narrative. "My dad had that same problem with the strip," recalls Schulz. "He was constantly reigning in Snoopy!"

To help balance the story, it was decided to include the entire collection of Peanuts characters, including some of the lesser-known members of the gang. "It was Steve [Martino] who suggested we expand the world by bringing in the characters that everyone wants to see and to broaden the scope and the message," recalls Craig Schulz.

At its core, the film is about everyday anxieties faced while growing up, going to school and the perceptions, be they true or misguided, people have about one another. "We took that theme and dramatically changed the overall tone of the movie," says Schulz, "which resulted in a stronger message, one that both adults and children can relate to."

For Martino, he needed to look no further than *A Charlie Brown Christmas* for inspiration on the construction of a story. "I've gone back to that special time and time again because I think it is a marvelous piece of storytelling," the director says.

In crafting the story, particular attention was paid to making sure each character received a proper introduction and point of reference. Fortunately for the filmmakers, they had a set of well-established characters with strong voices created by Charles Schulz.

"One of the challenges in animation is creating characters that are interesting and have depth, so that when you put them together, you're able to create interesting scenarios to drive comedy, emotion and a compelling story," explains Martino. "What Sparky has provided us with through all the years of the strip are really great characters. He wrote about universal topics that resonated with all of us, coming out of the voices of kids. They really are adults in children's bodies."

"Charlie Brown gets referred to as a loser all the time," laments Craig Schulz. "But in reality, Charlie Brown is a winner, and I don't think people see that. What they are going to see in the film is that Charlie Brown is a winner because he never gives up. We all lose a lot more than we win and who better than Charlie Brown to teach us that?"

All that's left now is to bring the characters to life!

Above: Charlie Brown gets knocked off pitcher's mound - *Final Digital Art*

DEFINING THE LOOK AND DESIGN OF
THE CHARACTERS

You're a Complicated Blockhead, Charlie Brown!

For lead character designer Sang Jun Lee, working on the film felt a bit like going back in time. "I grew up with the comic strip," recalls Lee. "When I started working on this film, I realized how simple it was and yet at the same time how hard it was. It wasn't until we went to Santa Rosa that I gained an understanding of Schulz's work and realized that there is so much information in his simple line work."

While it may seem simple on the surface, an understanding of Schulz's line and the meaning of each line was vital for the overall aesthetic of the movie, especially when translating a two-dimensional comic strip to 3D. "In 3D, we are adding more volume to the line," explains Lee. "Steve [Martino] wanted to make sure we had an understanding of the balances and the reasons for using a thin line versus thicker line and that ultimately makes the audience feel as though they are reading the comic strip; as if it were coming alive on the big screen."

The filmmakers knew early in the process that they had to settle on a consistent look that was representative of fifty years of Schulz's strip and style. "It was really fascinating to study his entire body of work," recalls director Steve Martino. As any casual reader of the strip knows, Charlie Brown and the entire cast of characters changed dramatically from 1950 to 2000. "We knew we had to settle on a definitive look for the design and models of the characters, but the overall question became, which Charlie Brown do we base our film on?" Martino continues. The careful selection of the best version of the characters was critical, because it would have to also ultimately be accepted by the movie's audience as the most authentic rendition of that character.

On advice given by the team at Schulz Creative Associates in Santa Rosa, the design team began searching the character designs from the 80s and 90s. The strips from this time frame were considered to be the "Classic" period by the group in Santa Rosa, and the characters had their most pleasing proportions and consistency in those two decades. But which of these examples of Charlie Brown would serve as the archetype to launch into modeling and into production?

Animation veteran and color designer Ric Sluiter suggested that a group be formed to pore over the thousands of panels from the classic period of the comic strip. It was the intention that this group, nicknamed the "Sparky Hero Group," would create a

Top: Charlie Brown - *Analysis by Nick Bruno*
Above: Charlie Brown height variations - *Assembled by Jason Sadler*

matrix for each character, selecting poses, expressions and angles of designs they felt best represented the characters. The group consisted of a mix of disciplines, including lead character designer Sang Jun Lee, supervising animators Nick Bruno and Scott Carroll, character modeling lead Shaun Cusick, character development supervisor Dan Barker, color designer Ric Sluiter, character designer Jason Sadler, associate production manager Angela Macias and art director Nash Dunnigan. Painstakingly reviewing every conceivable pose and angle that Schulz created, the group debated and then reached consensus for each character's attributes and what would ultimately

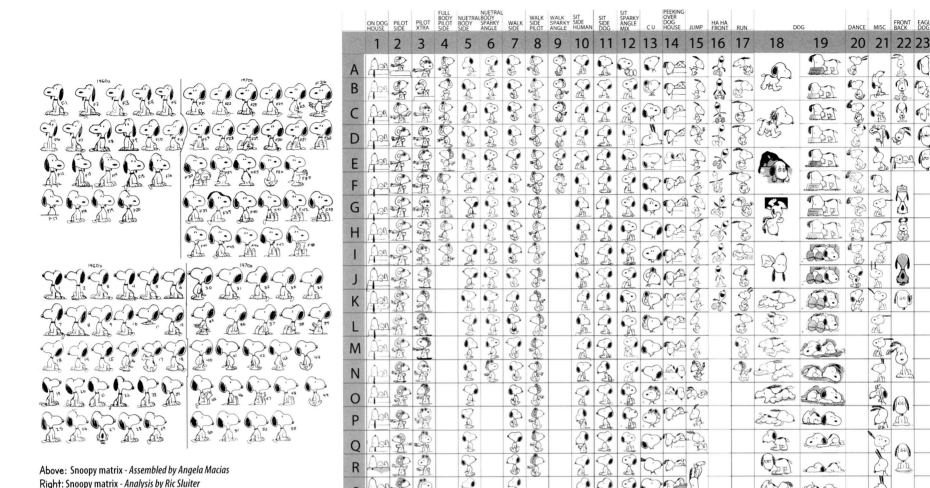

Above: Snoopy matrix - *Assembled by Angela Macias*
Right: Snoopy matrix - *Analysis by Ric Sluiter*

"*The most challenging part of animating Snoopy was trying to stay faithful to his many expressions. When Snoopy was calm and caring we'd make him look like the 1980s version that Sparky drew, but when he is more emotional or was in a battle with the Red Baron, Snoopy would change proportions and his actions would become much more zany, like the comics of the 1960s and 1970s. Balancing that wide range was extremely difficult to manage.*"

— **Jeff Gabor**, Lead Animator

inform their key poses for animation: ears, hair, noses, arms, profiles, etc.

"There is a consistency to the look of and the way Sparky drew the strip during that twenty-year period," observes Dunnigan. "It is the look that most everyone identifies with when they think of the Peanuts characters." It was that consistency in the shape language of the characters' design that resonated most with the artists. "One of the remarkable things about the Peanuts kids is that they are all constructed the same way," observes Lee. "If you look closely, you will notice there are only two head types,

one modeled after the Browns, the other after the Van Pelts."

"We knew that every decision made would have a ripple effect through the pipeline in every department," explains Martino. "Working together as a team was an invaluable process."

With the look of the characters decided, the team at Blue Sky spent nearly eight months working on what would end up serving as the basis for each of the characters: Charlie Brown's model and rig.

Above: Lucy, Snoopy, Linus, Sally, Franklin, Frieda - *Final Digital Art*
Right: Charlie Brown - *Final Digital Art*
Far right: Charlie Brown digital sculpt - *Model by Shaun Cusick*

You're Being Sculpted in 3D, Charlie Brown!

Just as a sculptor would evaluate a subject, so character modeling lead Shaun Cusick and his team of fourteen modelers studied the drawings of Charles Schulz, finding inspiration in the quality of his line. "We looked at the differences in Sparky's lines, from thick to thin, paying careful attention to how all the shapes came together," says Cusick. "The characters look so simple, but are so complex!"

Using ZBrush digital sculpting tools, Cusick's team translated the 2D character designs into 3D assets. "It is like working with 'meta-clay,'" explains Cusick. "During our design modeling phase, we take into consideration the technical specs, but it really is like you're sculpting in clay, only on a computer trying to find the essence of the character."

Once the design and modeling phase was completed, the team moved into the technical modeling phase, creating comprehensive 3D static meshes. During the entire process, there is cross-department collaboration to ensure consistency and continuity throughout the pipeline.

In a departure from the way Blue Sky has previously modeled characters, the team decided to use Charlie Brown's torso as the template for all the other kids. "Typically, we would create a character model that is one continuous model from head to toe," Cusick explains. "But for Charlie and all the other characters, we realized that since they basically all have the same body type, we could use one torso for all and just switch the heads and limbs. So we basically created modeling kits for this film."

What largely makes each of the Peanuts characters instantly recognizable in silhouette is the unique shape language of each character's hairstyle. Since each character has idiosyncrasies with their hair, the modeling team had to evaluate each one and figure out both technically and aesthetically how the model would hold up throughout the pipeline.

"Their hair was very tricky," admits Cusick. "Their hairstyles are very iconic, so in most cases, we had to create multiple hairdos for each character, based on character views from the front, profile and three-quarter. Everyone knows what Lucy's bob looks like, especially from profile, so we applied a scaling ratio to her hair."

"Peppermint Patty was a real challenge for us," continues Cusick. "When you look at her from the side, it looks like she has curtains that come across, so we had to take multiple angles into consideration."

While the Charlie Brown template worked for all the other kids, it certainly would not work for Snoopy or Woodstock. However, when you look closely, Snoopy and Woodstock share a similar facial structure and shape, so it made sense to approach the characters in the same manner.

"Adam McMahon was the modeler for both Snoopy and Woodstock and he did a great job," says Cusick. There are basically six different variations of Snoopy in 3D: the two profiles, the front ("flounder eyes"), the "helicopter" (flying with twirling ears), the classic "inverted bowling pin/bottlenose" pose and the Flying Ace pose with the goggles. "Basically, he's like a Picasso in 3D," Cusick jokes.

"For five of the poses, it is all the same head [model]," explains Cusick. "But we had to make the nose, eyes and ears all separate so they could move across Snoopy's head and work in frame." The bowling pin/bottlenose Snoopy pose is a separate model. "That pose required a lot of snappy, quick movements which required a completely different model."

Left: WWI Flying Ace - *Final Digital Art*
Right: Woodstock - *Final Digital Art*

Happiness is a Working Rig

Once the characters were designed and modeled, the task of creating rigs fell to character development supervisor Sabine Heller and her team. "Think of a rig as basically a skeleton or a puppet," explains Heller. "Our department takes the 3D models and assigns controls to the various 'puppet strings,' giving the animators the ability to move the character."

"The hardest part of our job is that we don't know if we're doing it right until we test it," says rigging supervisor Justin Leach. "We went through a lot of iterations with the animation department, testing the controls, even trying to break it. Depending on the outcome, we would either tweak, rebuild or – thankfully – move forward with an approved rig."

While it took nearly eight months defining the look of Charlie Brown and the other characters, the rigging team spent nearly eighteen months developing the rigs for Charlie Brown – which would serve as the template for the other kids – and Snoopy. "Of all the films at Blue Sky, this was definitely the most difficult one we've ever done," says Leach.

For the team, one of the biggest challenges in creating a rig based on characters from a comic strip is that the laws of physics basically do not apply. "In the real world, the shape of a human's face doesn't change as they move from side to side," explains Heller. "But that's not the way [Schulz] drew the characters, so in the world of Peanuts, when a character turns, the shape and positioning of their features change."

"When it came to Snoopy," adds Leach, "if you really look closely, you realize that his eyes are on the same side of his face. You just don't think about it, it just looks right. It is very hard to make that look correct in 3D and stay within the guidelines of dimension and physical space."

Working closely with the animators to convert the characters from 2D to 3D, Heller led a team of character technical directors/riggers to create camera view dependent rigs that would allow for those variances when the characters would transition from pose to pose, front to side to three-quarter. "We created rigs that allowed their noses, ears and other features to actually move across the model," says Heller.

Since the characters heads and bodies were modeled with separate pieces of geometry, much like a golf ball on a tee, the rigging department developed a hybrid rig that was combined with a tool that allowed for smooth transitions between two surfaces. But having a character's head separate from their body presented new transmittance (how light passes through translucent material) and lighting challenges for the materials

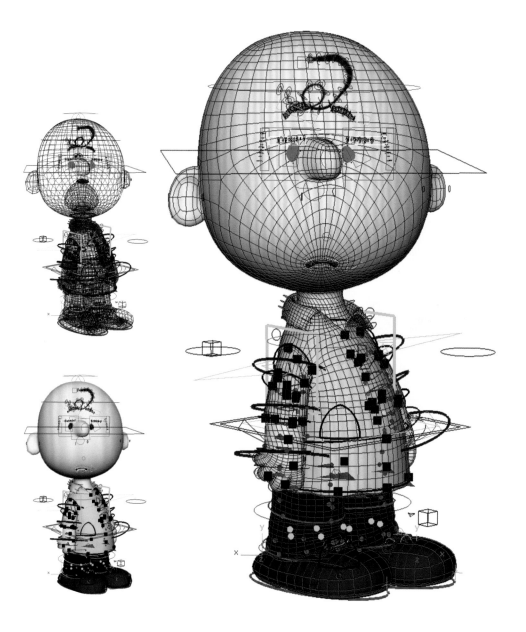

department, led by lead materials technical director Nikki Tomaino and materials supervisor Brian Hill. They are responsible, in this particular instance, for the way light passes through a character's skin.

"We had to work closely with research and development when it came to the intersecting points of the pieces of geometry," explains Tomaino. "The way [Blue Sky co-founder and head of research and development] Carl Ludwig built our proprietary transmittance model was based on real-world sub-surface scattering, so that when light enters an object it

Above: Charlie Brown rig

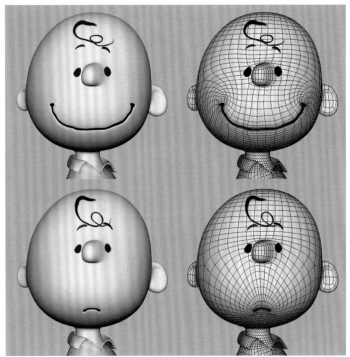

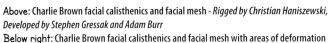

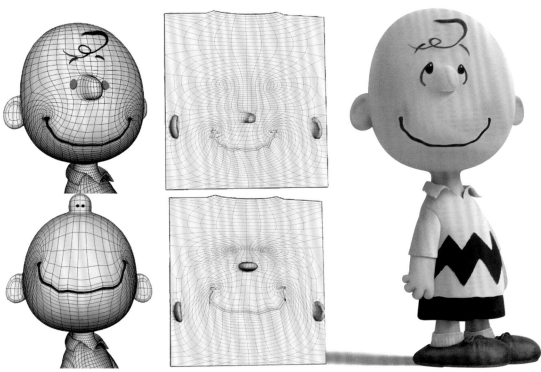

Above: Charlie Brown facial calisthenics and facial mesh - *Rigged by Christian Haniszewski, Developed by Stephen Gressak and Adam Burr*
Below right: Charlie Brown facial calisthenics and facial mesh with areas of deformation
- *Rigged by Christian Haniszewski, Developed by Stephen Gressak and Adam Burr*

Above: Charlie Brown - *Final Digital Art*

is going to be able to determine how thick or thin it is," adds Hill. "But with two pieces of geometry those patterns will be interrupted and look different and off model."

Working with Ludwig, Tomaino, Hill and their team essentially had to rebuild the transmittance program to ensure seamless blending of light between each character's head and neckline. "Essentially it was like rebuilding the wheel," says Tomaino

Throughout the development and design process, each department realized that every character had their own unique set of challenges.

"They look so simple, but yet are among the most complex to go through our pipeline," says Dunnigan. Adds CG supervisor Rob Cavaleri, "When the character holds an expression for a beat, completely still between the action, you ponder their every movement. You ask yourself, 'What are they thinking about? What will they do next?' It brings you closer to the characters."

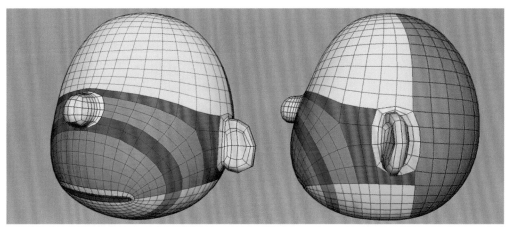

Above: Concept art for characters - *Design and Color by Sang Jun Lee, Ric Sluiter, Vincent Nguyen, Robert MacKenzie and José Manuel Fernandez Oli*

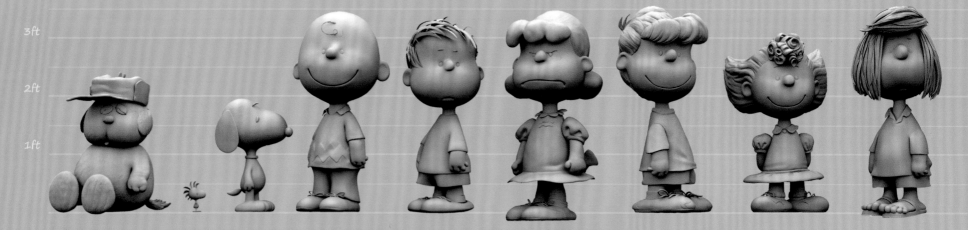

Above: Digital sculpts for character development - *Models by Shaun Cusick, Adam McMahon, Ian Bukard, Motoko Wada, Cleveland Hibbert, Christian Haniszewski, Sabina Suarez and Rizwana Rangwala*

Above: Line-up of 'hero' characters - *Assembled by Sang Jun Lee*

CHARLIE BROWN

WHENEVER I FEEL REALLY ALONE, I JUST SIT AND STARE INTO THE NIGHT SKY. I'VE ALWAYS THOUGHT THAT ONE OF THOSE STARS WAS MY STAR, AND AT MOMENTS LIKE THIS, I KNOW THAT MY STAR WILL ALWAYS BE THERE FOR ME, LIKE A COMFORTING VOICE SAYING, "DON'T GIVE UP, KID."

To say that "Good ol' Charlie Brown" holds a unique position in pop culture would be an understatement. He has the illustrious distinction of being the only Peanuts character to appear in both the first comic strip on October 2, 1950 and the last strip on February 13, 2000. Despite his less-than-stellar track record as a baseball manager, his inability to fly a kite or kick a football, through it all Charlie Brown never gives up. His eternal optimism gives us hope and that has made him undeniably relatable to readers all over the world.

"Everybody's got a little piece of Charlie Brown in them," observes Martino. "What's great about him is that he operates on such an extreme level, which always makes you feel better about your 'Charlie-Brown-ness.' We've all been in those awkward situations and we've all had failures. He teaches us a wonderful thing in that in the midst of all that, you can pick yourself up and try again, so it was very important for us to capture that spirit in his expressions."

As the team began the process of refining details for each of the characters' looks, they turned their attention to one of Charlie Brown's most defining features: his hair. Or lack thereof.

Left: Charlie Brown - *Final Digital Art*

Tying the features together correctly, gives the model dimension!

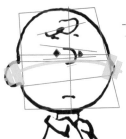

- assymmetry
- features rest on barbell
  implied by heavy weighted ears
- wood staple nose lifts up
- **triangle diamond eyes**
- angles and scale suggest
  forced perspective

Dimensional!

- too symmetrical
- perky ears disrupt flow
- flat bottomed nose
- **mirrored eyes**
- flattened angles

Flat...

All design elements are heaviest just south of the midpoint. No head shape is symmetrial or spherical in any way, always some form of skewed trapezoid.

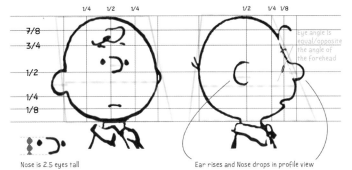

Nose is 2.5 eyes tall

Ear rises and Nose drops in profile view

Above: Charlie Brown head - *Analysis by Nick Bruno and Scott Carroll*

Above: Charlie Brown facial expressions with Sparky sketch - *Design by Sang Jun Lee*

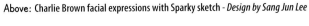

Above: Charlie Brown standing and running head axis study - *Developed by Michael Reed and Sabine Heller, Rigged by Christian Hanszewski*

Left: Charlie Brown -
Final Digital Art

CHARLIE BROWN'S HAIR THROUGH THE DECADES

1952

1990

this seems to be a cowlick with some weight which could be suggested in the frontal view

slight suggestion of overlapping form, which suggest a 'poof' of hair

side view

SURPRISE/WORRY

axis

POSE_Worried_Internal

axis

wider than neutral pose

axis

POSE_Ground_SitUp

NEUTRAL

FACE_Analyzing

axis

axis

POSE_OpenArms.jpg

SAD/DEPRESSED

FACE_OpenShock

Bottom of curl is parallel to eyes

first stroke of hair is curved and broken at an 'elbow'

axis

POSE_Sit_Onphone

HAPPY

FACE_Smile

axis

FACE_Smile_OpenMouth

sometimes the loop is flat on top

This page: Charlie Brown's hair - *Analysis by Nash Dunnigan*

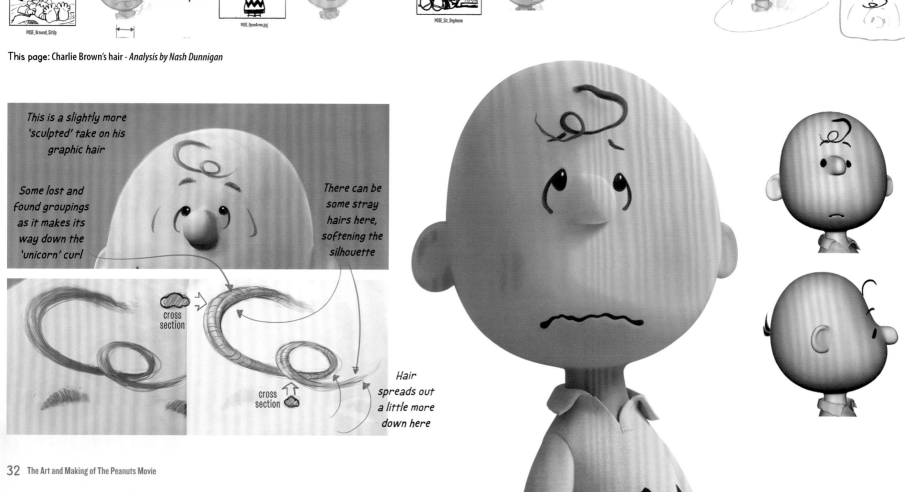

This is a slightly more 'sculpted' take on his graphic hair

Some lost and found groupings as it makes its way down the 'unicorn' curl

There can be some stray hairs here, softening the silhouette

cross section

cross section

Hair spreads out a little more down here

So just what exactly is the curlicue, loop-de-loop swirl that rests just above Charlie Brown's forehead called? "I just call it his hair," says Martino with a smile. "But what little hair he has in that loop is full of personality," continues the director. "The way Schulz drew his hair would echo Charlie Brown's emotions. It would move and reinforce his own expressions."

According to Charlie Brown's stylist – aka fur supervisor – Jon Campbell, 219 strands of hair were created for his iconic swirl/loop/curl.

"All of his hairs are wound up into a bundle," explains Campbell. "We knew we could not just give Charlie Brown a single hair. No matter how the hair is rendered, it would only be a pixel wide, so that is why we bundled a large number of hairs that we squeezed, straightened and relaxed just right to basically reproduce the ebb and flow of Schulz's pen line."

Because Schulz drew the hair loop differently each time, Campbell knew he needed to provide the animators with enough flexibility to achieve the desired results. "If we were to take a hair and groom it into a curve, it will basically be stuck in that position," he explains. "So instead of grooming his hair into a loop-de-loop, we groomed it straight out, like a unicorn, and rigged it, allowing the animators to control it." Campbell compares Charlie Brown's hair rig to that of a spring coil: "You have no idea how long a spring actually is until you uncoil it," he says. "Proportionally, when uncoiled, Charlie Brown's hair is nearly two feet long!"

In a nod to the spring coil reference, Martino cites a very subtle Easter egg (an oblique reference or in-joke) in the film: "The wire sculpture that Charlie Brown makes by mistake looks exactly like his hair loop."

"The most challenging thing about animating Charlie Brown was creating a performance that was original but still stayed true to the Peanuts world. With all the years of comics and TV specials, there is a lot of source material to study. I always tried to reference that material as much as possible, so that Charlie Brown's actions and choices stayed grounded in what had already been established."

— **Steve Vanseth**, Character Animator

Above: Charlie Brown's wire sculpture - *Design and Color by Tyler Carter*
Right: Charlie Brown in the nurse's office - *Design by Tyler Carter, Painting by Ric Sluiter*

SNOOPY

Joe Cool. World Famous Author. Flying Ace. Best Friend. Everyone has their favorite Snoopy persona. Since his first appearance in the October 4, 1950 strip, Snoopy has continued to enthrall, amaze and entertain audiences around the world.

Bringing the beloved beagle to life in 3D presented Blue Sky Studios with their biggest challenge to date. "Snoopy is by far the most complex character to ever go through the studio's pipeline," says production manager Anthony Nisi.

One of the biggest problems to solve with regard to Snoopy's design were his eyes, particularly their placement. "If you look at Snoopy's profile, three-quarter and from the front, it is the exact same shape," notes character designer Sang Jun Lee. Adds Dunnigan, "He basically has flounder-eyes, and in CG that is a nearly impossible riddle to solve."

Riddle or no riddle, the team was determined to crack the look of the beagle's eyes. First they placed Snoopy's eyes where one would expect them to be. But the design never looked right. According to Dunnigan, "The look fell apart. So the animators decided to embrace the limitation and put two eyes on the side of his head, which turned out to be a monumental decision."

While the two-eyes/flounder-eyes approach worked creatively and aesthetically, the decision started a chain reaction throughout production. "We literally broke our pipeline on the film," says Dunnigan.

Left: Snoopy Dance -
Final Digital Art

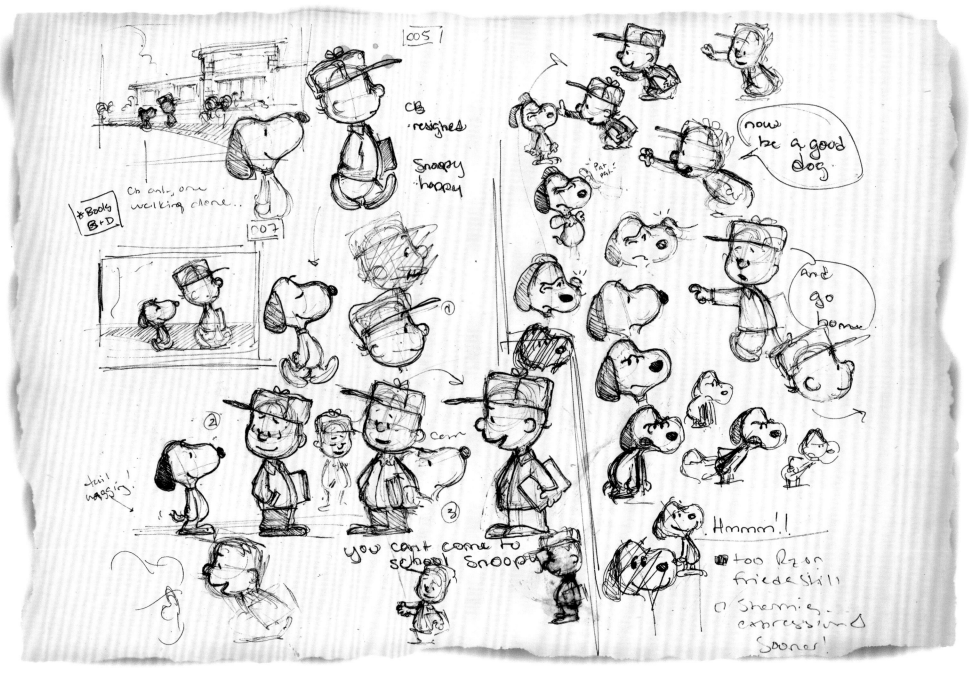

Above: Animation sketch pose planning: Charlie Brown pats Snoopy on the head and heads into school - *Thumbnails by Lisa Allen*

  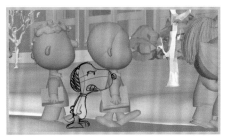 

Above: Animation sketch pose planning and blocking - *Thumbnails and Animation by Lisa Allen*

"The decision had repercussions in rigging, animation and especially lighting. You can't light a 3D object that has a beautiful exterior shape and place two eyes on one side. As soon as you attempt to realistically light the face, the cheat of the eyes becomes evident."

In a more traditional film, lighting artists would add subtle reflections of surrounding sets and highlights to a character's iris to add life to the eyes. But as lighting supervisor Jeeyun Sung Chisholm explains, lighting the eyes of the Peanuts characters proved to be a balancing act between realistic details and making those details look like they belong in the streamlined design of each character. "After many iterations of tests, we decided that Snoopy looks best with simple specular highlights on his flat eyes," she says. "Probably the biggest challenge was to make the shape of the highlights follow the ever-changing shape of the eyes that deform with each new pose."

Balancing the color of Snoopy's fur against a winter background full of snow was another particular challenge. "Even though it looks simple, we went through so many concepts," says Chisholm. Ultimately, the lighting team settled on a platinum-gray-white shade for Snoopy, which subtly sets him apart from the snow.

"We're cutting the shading at one third of Snoopy's height," explains Chisholm. "At any given frame, in the bottom third you will start to see roll-off and see a little bit of gray, which we are calling platinum-gray." The lighting team was constantly making adjustments between the warmer and cooler color values of Snoopy's white fur based on his placement within the scene for any given frame.

To alleviate concerns that Snoopy would be too uniformly white, the lighting team decided to start using a little less shading in some areas. For example, to accentuate his eyes "We ended up making the center area next to his eyes the brightest white and then the edges slightly shaded," says Chisholm, "so you can see that at the edge of the silhouette there's a little bit of roll-off." Spotlights were placed around his eyes so that the center area reads a little brighter.

Equally important was to make sure the audience could see the obvious definition in the beagle's arms and feet. So spotlights were placed in the shots to ensure an even amount of light would hit Snoopy's arms and legs both when static and in motion.

Because Snoopy comes across as one continuous smooth shape, spotlights were also placed to make sure there were consistent transitions anywhere on his body from frame to frame.

"The lighting team did an incredible job with Snoopy," praises Dunnigan. "The final rendered look is very convincing. We were at first concerned that his fur might 'swim' underneath the eyes, but even our compositing team worked on the construction of the character, helping to pull all the final elements together."

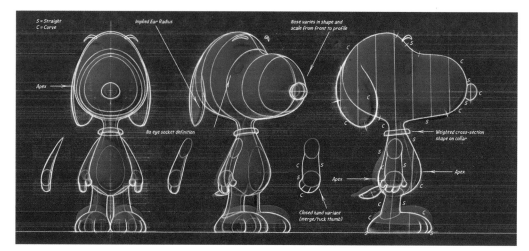

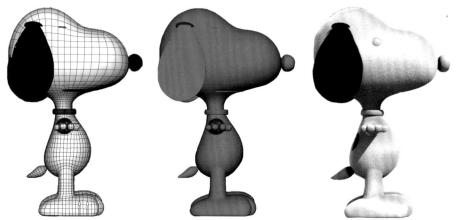

Top: Snoopy turnaround - *Design by Jason Sadler*
Above: Snoopy side view: mesh, model and fur - *Model by Adam McMahon*

Above: Snoopy and Woodstock sledding down library hill - *Final Digital Art*

"Aside from the Flying Ace, of all of Snoopy's personas, I think my favorite has to be when he would imitate animals, especially the vulture, which was always hilarious."

— Paul Feig, Producer

Left: Concept painting for Snoopy as Flying Ace
- *Design by José Manuel Fernández Oli*
Below: The Flying Ace vs. the Red Baron over airshow
- *Design and Color by José Manuel Fernández Oli*

They're Called Periwinkles, Charlie Brown!

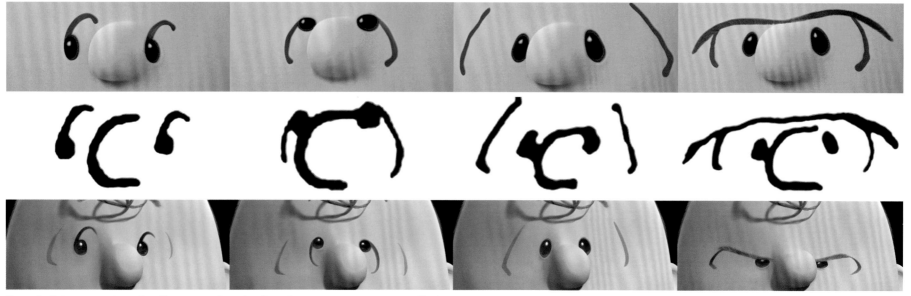

Above: Charlie Brown expression analysis: First row: *Final Digital Art;* Second row: Comic art - *by Charles Schulz;* Third row: *Concept art by Sang Jun Lee, Rigging by Sabine Heller*

Of all the challenges presented to the entire crew, one of the most difficult to get right was the characters' eyes. For all intents and purposes, they basically are a pair of black dots, and yet Schulz was able to convey an enormous amount of emotion with them. Whether the desired emotion was happiness, surprise, frustration or indifference, Schulz was able to convey expressions in the most subtle ways with just a stroke of his pen.

In researching the characters, lead character designer Sang Jun Lee figured out the implied ellipse (or curve) of the eyes if the characters had a sclera (the white outer membrane of the eye). "Schulz had an implied construction in his drawing, with '6s and 9s' alluding or nodding to an eye structure," says Lee. "The 6s represent direction to the left or to the right, the 9s typically represent an upward look or expression, and the 'periwinkles' are used to emphasis emotion."

So what exactly are 6s, 9s and periwinkles? "Basically, the 6s and 9s represent the outline of an eyelid," explains Lee, "and periwinkles are what we nicknamed the wrinkles around and above the eyes of the characters."

"Throughout all our research, we gained an enormous appreciation for Sparky's drafting and cartooning ability," adds art director Nash Dunnigan. "We discovered an underlying facial mask of expressions that he always utilized, which at first glance you wouldn't necessarily notice. Lee and the animation supervisors deciphered the relationships between all the pieces and parts, the eyebrows and eyes, operating as one unit."

Early in the pre-production phase, the filmmakers realized that traditional eye rig setups would not allow the animators to achieve the desired functionality and look.

"After exploring multiple approaches, including traditional eyes with sockets, we settled on a sliding eye setup, which provided the materials department with controls to adjust the rendered look and custom plug-ins featuring iris and pupil controls," explains character development supervisor Sabine Heller.

Just as the position of the noses and ears shifts when moving from front to profile views, the eye shapes change as well, which meant adding an "eye camera projection functionality." That basically created the illusion of a consistent eye shape whatever the position of the eye on the character's face.

For the periwinkles, also called expression lines, the character design required that the lines integrate with the skin. To accomplish this, the rigging and materials departments developed "poseable" textures – periwinkles – that could be controlled by the animators, which in turn would allow the materials department to properly integrate the expressions into the texture of the character's skin. "Since the animation style and the technical implementation were so closely connected, we literally had to reinvent our pipeline," says Heller.

That reinvention frequently meant thinking outside the box, leading to some very creative problem solving. Because of the technical issues the animators faced with Snoopy's rig, they realized early on in the process that they would not be able to animate Snoopy's mouth from one side to the other. A challenge which lead animator

FACE VOCABULARY

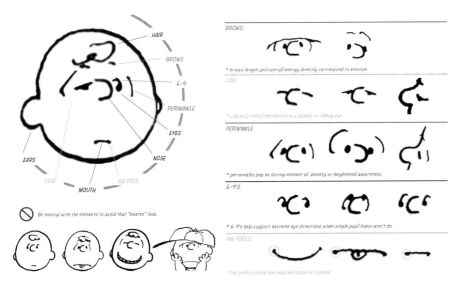

Above: Charlie Brown 'face vocabulary' - *Analysis by Nick Bruno and Scott Carroll*

THE EYE MASK

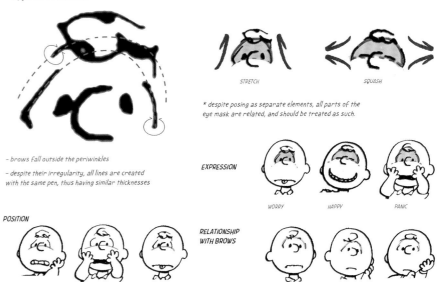

Above: Charlie Brown 'eye mask' analysis - *Design by Sang Jun Lee, Analysis by Nick Bruno and Scott Carroll*

Jeff Gabor set out to answer.

"I was working on facial expressions one day and just got frustrated that we were giving up on something so iconic to Snoopy," recalls Gabor. "So I took his periwinkle and literally took it down and around to continue the other side of his mouth. I had no idea how or if this would even render."

To the team's delight, they discovered that Snoopy's mouth rig and his periwinkles could be used interchangeably to achieve the desired result by changing the thickness of the line. "Sometimes, we were even able to hide the mouth rig entirely and use the periwinkles to build a smile," adds Gabor, "and other times, we would use a periwinkle to complete the other side of his smile."

"Basically, everyone got tired of saying 'a pair of wrinkles' – or 'parentheses' – so we decided to settle on the term 'periwinkles.'"

— Steve Martino, Director

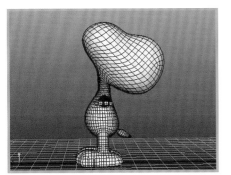
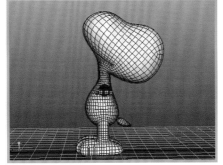
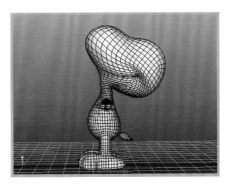
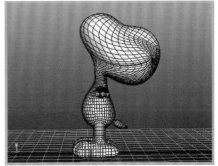

Above: Snoopy mesh neck and smile deformation test - *Rigging by Ignacio Barrios, Developed by Ferris Webby*

LINUS VAN PELT

LISTEN, CHARLIE BROWN. IGNORING WHAT MY SISTER LUCY SAYS HAS ENABLED ME TO MAKE IT THIS FAR IN LIFE.

Charlie Brown's loyal and trustworthy friend Linus made his first appearance as the baby brother of Lucy on September 19, 1952, but did not actually speak until 1954. Over the years, Schulz progressed his age to match that of the other characters. Whether on the baseball field (where Linus plays second base), at the neighborhood wall or showing unwavering faith in the Great Pumpkin, Linus is always there for Charlie Brown. "You like to think that sometimes you might have just a little bit of that wisdom that Linus has," says director Steve Martino. "I always loved that about him. Here's the kid with the security blanket, but he possesses wisdom years beyond any of the other kids."

Although Linus's trusty blanket does not take on a personality in the movie like it does in the specials, multiple rigs were created so that the blanket could be animated and posed to do whatever the animators needed it to do. "There was the classic pose of Linus sucking his thumb while holding the blanket," recalls supervising animator Nick Bruno, "crumbled on the floor, over his head like a shepherd, and being dragged along on the ground."

Right: Linus and his security blanket - *Final Digital Art*

Top row: *Analysis by Jason Sadler*; Bottom row: *Design by Sang Jun Lee*

"I think Linus is my favorite character. He has insecurities that he overcomes in his own unique way. Instead of hiding them, he embraces them, and does so with intelligence, humor and class."

— **David Mei**, Modeling Supervisor

Above: Linus concept art - *Design by Sang Jun Lee*

Above: Peanuts, December 30, 1990

Left: Linus and security blanket - *Rigging by James Gu*

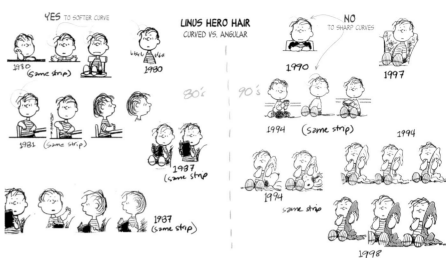

YES TO SOFTER CURVE

LINUS HERO HAIR
CURVED VS. ANGULAR

NO
TO SHARP CURVES

Above: Linus hair comparison - *Analysis by Nash Dunnigan*
Left: Linus in the pumpkin patch - *Sketchbook drawing by Steve Martino*

Above: Linus hair analysis - *Design and Painting by Sang Jun Lee and Robert MacKenzie*

Above: Linus hair study with and without lights - *Final Digital Art*

Above: Snoopy grabs Linus's blanket on the skating pond - *Final Digital Art*
Below right: Linus skating and celebrating - *Final Digital Art*

For fur supervisor Jon Campbell, Linus's hair, or more accurately, lack thereof, proved rather challenging when it came to defining the character's look.

"In some of the reference from the strip, he basically just has three ribbons or strands of hair," says Campbell. "Translating those ribbons into a full head of hair became our problem to solve."

Turning to the work of Tom Everhart, the team's primary goal was to stay true to Schulz's pen line. By closely examining the work of Everhart, the artists were able to fill in the blanks, or in this case, hairs.

"We explored a lot of iterations on Linus, settling on three layers of different kinds of hair," Campbell says. "Two layers are actually two varying degrees of fuzz with a final layer of different lengths and sizes of strands rigged in a similar manner to Charlie Brown's hair."

LUCY VAN PELT

OH, CHARLIE BROWWWWWN.
I'LL HOLD THE FOOTBALL
AND YOU KICK IT...

For years, that sing-songy lilt in Lucy's voice as she tossed a football in the air, taunting our hero, has pretty much defined her character. Charlie Brown's ultimate foil, Lucille "Lucy" Van Pelt made her first appearance as a toddler on March 3, 1952. By 1954, however, Schulz had aged her to be Charlie Brown's contemporary and the two have been going at it ever since. Lucy plays right field on Charlie Brown's baseball team. She has never caught a fly ball. Despite her brash, overbearing and sometimes all-too-honest observations, she does have a softer side. It was Lucy who actually said the now-familiar phase "Happiness is a warm puppy" in the April 4, 1960 comic strip.

"She genuinely likes Charlie Brown and cares about him," observes director Steve Martino. "When she gives him advice at her psychiatric booth, she may do so in a funny way, but it's coming from a place where she's really trying to help him. She sees the world through her own filter and fully believes that is the only way to see the world."

Lucy's unique point of view, sense of humor and ability to cut to the chase are front and center in the film, and for some, it was a chance to rediscover just how funny she can be. "In researching the strip and

Right: Lucy - Final Digital Art

exploring the characters, I had forgotten just how funny Lucy as a character really is," says producer Michael Travers. "Her certainty that she's always right and her 'my way or the highway' attitude, while being completely wrong, end up being some of the funniest moments in the film – Lucy just being Lucy."

Charlie Brown and Snoopy aside, perhaps one of the most recognizable silhouettes of all the characters is the shape language of Lucy's hair. But keeping her iconic bob on model was a challenge.

Above: Lucy 'Sparky hero' page - *Analysis by Jason Sadler*

Lucy's hat is made of a fuzzy felt material that absorbs a lot of light

Right: Lucy's springtime and winter wardrobe - *Design and Color by Robert MacKenzie and Tyler Carter*

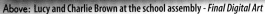

Above: Lucy and Charlie Brown at the school assembly - *Final Digital Art*

Above: Lucy prepares for her triple axle - *Final Digital Art*

This page: Charlie Brown attempts to kick the football as Lucy pulls it away - *Design and Color by Tyler Carter*

Below: Peanuts, October 20, 1996

"The bob is always dominant on the opposite side to where she looks," Martino explains. "We designed the objects of her hair so that when she goes from one Sparky-view pose to another, the objects will move and snap in place to follow her eyeline."

Because of the sheer volume of hair on Lucy (and other characters such as Schroeder, Marcie and Peppermint Patty), the crew wanted to avoid the dreaded "helmet hair" look. Explains Jon Campbell, fur supervisor, "We purposely added flyaway hairs on Lucy and other characters to not only avoid helmet hair, but to emphasize the Sparky line. These are messy kids."

SCHROEDER

BEETHOVEN IS **IT**, CLEAR AND SIMPLE!! DO YOU UNDERSTAND?

Child music prodigy Schroeder made his first appearance on May 3, 1951 and is Charlie Brown's reliable catcher on the ball field. Over the years, Schulz would include a number of musical references in Peanuts for die-hard fans and music lovers, painstakingly recreating actual passages of music for the strip. Although Beethoven is clearly Schroeder's idol, the first piece of music depicted in the strip and that Schulz transcribed was Sergei Rachmaninoff's Prelude in G minor. Like all of the great masters of music – Beethoven, Bach, Brahms – Schroeder is simply known as "Schroeder." Even his house number, 1770 James Street, is a nod to the year Beethoven was born.

When it came time to develop the rig for the musical genius, the team realized they would need to re-imagine and reconfigure the overall functionality of the rig and controls.

Below: Schroeder plays the piano -
Final Digital Art

"He was extremely complicated," says art director Nash Dunnigan. "When Schroeder sits to play the piano, his torso elongates and it almost looks like his back is broken and he's cantilevered across the piano." To compensate, controls were added to the rig that allowed animators to seamlessly transition the character between his iconic poses. "If Schroeder were to go from sitting at the piano to standing without those controls, he would be nearly three times his normal height," adds rigging supervisor Justin Leach.

Below: Schroeder and Lucy at the piano - *Design and Color by Ric Sluiter*

Below: Peanuts, October 4, 1983

Schroeder Stripes

Painted over current material renders

9 by 3 stripes   10 by 4 stripes

current   9 by 3 stripes   10 by 4 stripes

Standing
6 Black stripes
*includes collar

Sitting Pose
9 Black stripes
*includes collar

Above: Schroeder's stripe count on shirt - *Design by Ric Sluiter, Analysis by Tyler Carter*

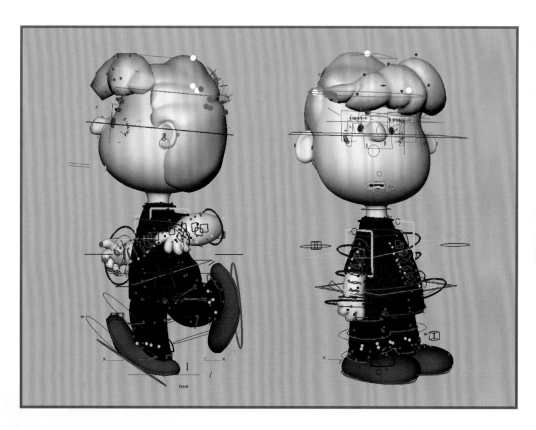

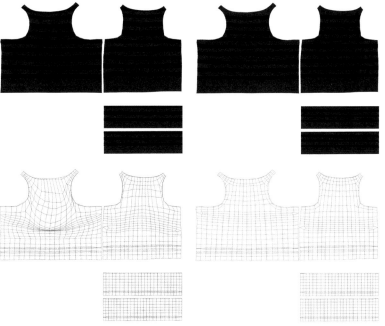

Left: Schroeder's animation rig
Above: Schroeder stripes variation on shirt material

"We knew this pose would be hard to achieve and a challenge for our animation and materials teams," recalls character development supervisor Sabine Heller, "so we tested it early on."

When Schroeder sits at his piano, the pose proved so extreme that the materials department needed to create a custom UV simulation for his iconic striped purple-and-black shirt.

"We are essentially blending two UVs so that there is a seamless transition from six stripes in his shirt when standing, to nine stripes when he's sitting at the piano," says lead materials technical director Nikki Tomaino.

"We had to work with our character simulation team to relax the UVs, or the matrix that assigns values between the various points of the geometry, so that no matter how extreme the model's movement, it had to match the texture on the surface of his shirt," explains rigging supervisor Justin Leach. "His mesh was considerably compromised, and yet we managed to keep the shirt from stretching."

Supervising animator Nick Bruno compares the simulation to that of Silly Putty being stretched. "When you have an image on Silly Putty and stretch it, the images distorts," he explains. "What a UV simulation does is keep the image intact, even though it is being distorted to extremes."

Above: Schroeder in goal at the skating pond - *Final Digital Art*
Left: Schroeder skating - *Final Digital Art*

SALLY BROWN

THE FAME THAT COMES WITH INTELLECTUAL SUPERIORITY CAN BE VERY FLEETING.

Since making her first appearance in the August 23, 1959 strip as the new baby sister of Charlie Brown, Sally Brown has endeared herself to readers over the years with her devotion to her "Sweet Babboo" Linus, quirky take on philosophy and the unintentional but humorous malapropisms she delivers in her school reports. Throughout the movie, Sally provides many humorous moments, including a cowgirl talent show act and a stint as a marketer hawking Charlie Brown-themed merchandise.

Right: Sally - *Final Digital Art*

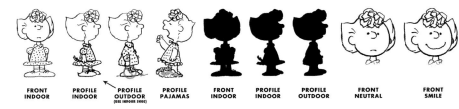

FRONT INDOOR | PROFILE INDOOR | PROFILE OUTDOOR (USE INDOOR SHOE) | PROFILE PAJAMAS | FRONT INDOOR | PROFILE INDOOR | PROFILE OUTDOOR | FRONT NEUTRAL | FRONT SMILE

Above: *Analysis by Jason Sadler, Design by Sang Jun Lee*
Below: Peanuts, August 23, 1960

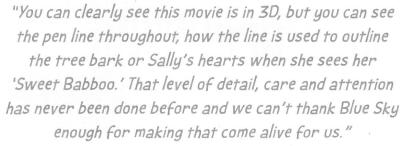

"You can clearly see this movie is in 3D, but you can see the pen line throughout, how the line is used to outline the tree bark or Sally's hearts when she sees her 'Sweet Babboo.' That level of detail, care and attention has never been done before and we can't thank Blue Sky enough for making that come alive for us."

— Bryan Schulz, Writer/Producer

Above: Sally sees Linus at the dance - *Final Digital Art*

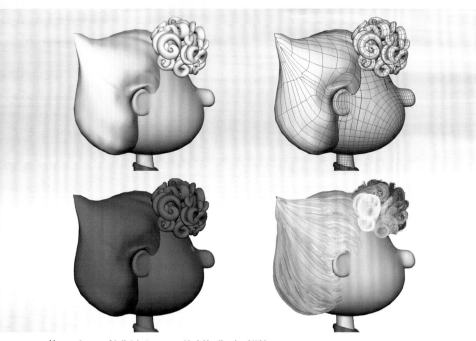

Above: Stages of Sally's hair groom - *Model by Cleveland Hibbert*
Above right: Concept art for Sally's hair - *Design by Ric Sluiter*

"All the pieces and parts of each character had to support each angle, which is not typically the norm in animation. In the case of Sally, the angles of her hair presented a unique problem to solve. Is that a parting in her hair? A wedge? We nicknamed them 'horns,' and they bounce!"

— **Nash Dunnigan**, Art Director

Above: Sally's hair concept art - *Design by Ric Sluiter*

Above: Sally digital sculpt - *Model by Shaun Cusick*

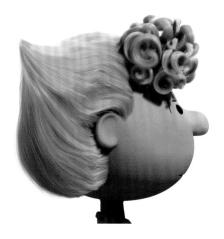

Above: Sally's final hair groom - *Final Digital Art*

Above: Concept art for Sally - *Design by Sang Jun Lee*

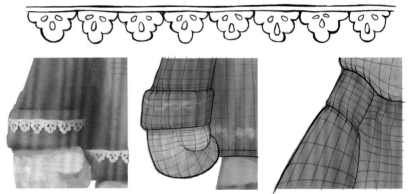

Above: Concept art for Sally's winter coat and decoration - *Design by Kevin Yang*

Left: Sally - *Final Digital Art*
Right: Concept art for Sally's winter coat - *Design by Kevin Yang*

PEPPERMINT PATTY

> HEY, LOOK AT THAT FUNNY LOOKING KID WITH THE BIG NOSE.

Inspired by a dish of Peppermint Pattie candy sitting on Charles Schulz's desk, Patricia "Peppermint Patty" Reichardt made her first appearance in the strip on August 22, 1966 and quickly became one of the most popular characters of the series. As the manager of the rival baseball team that routinely clobbers Charlie Brown's team, Peppermint Patty and "Chuck" share a passion for the game.

Peppermint Patty's personal hair regime is in direct contrast to the perfectly coiffed hairstyles of Patty and Violet. "Peppermint Patty is the definition of roll out of bed and go to school," jokes director Steve Martino.

But bringing order to the chaos of her locks was not an easy task. To accentuate the shapes that define her style, the team basically created "curtains" of hair for the character by placing negative space in the clumps of her hair to replicate Schulz's pen line.

Right: Peppermint Patty - *Final Digital Art*

Like Lucy, Peppermint Patty also has an iconic shape above her forehead in the form of what was dubbed a "football." Great care was taken when lighting the character to avoid sharp, contrasting shadows that could potentially fall across her face. "We made certain to not cover her eyes and made any shadow a bit lighter," says lighting supervisor Jeeyun Sung Chisholm.

Right: Animation pose planning - *Thumbnail and Animation by Graham Silva*

TOP PICKS	1	2	3	4	5	6	7
HAIR	✓	✓	✓			✓	✓
BANGS			✓		✓		✓
EYES					✓		✓
NOSE				✓	✓	✓	✓
FRECKLES	✓						✓
PROFILE	✓					✓	✓
MOUTH						✓	✓

TOP PICKS	1	2	3	4	5	6	7	8	9	10
HAIR					✓	✓	✓		✓	✓
BANGS					✓	✓	✓			
EYES		✓								
NOSE	✓		✓		✓					
FRECKLES				✓	✓					
PROFILE				✓	✓					

"BEST OF" COMP — INSIDE LINE — OUTSIDE LINE — INBETWEEN LINE — INSIDE LINE — OUTSIDE LINE — INBETWEEN LINE — INBETWEEN LINE WITH OUTSIDE LINE FOR HAIR *with Jun adjusted eye* — "BEST OF" COMP — INSIDE LINE — OUTSIDE LINE — INBETWEEN LINE — INSIDE LINE — OUTSIDE LINE — INBETWEEN LINE — ORIGINAL FACE LINES — CLEAN FACE LINES — WITH SCLERA — WITH A LITTLE SUGAR

Above: Peppermint Patty 'Sparky hero' - *Analysis by Ric Sluiter*

Above: Peppermint Patty 'Sparky hero' analysis and concept art - *Design by Ric Sluiter*

Right: Peppermint Patty animation pose planning - *Thumbnail and Animation by Eric Prah*
Below: Peppermint Patty final rendered poses - *Final Digital Art*

Below: Peppermint Patty and Marcie at the skating pond - *Final Digital Art*

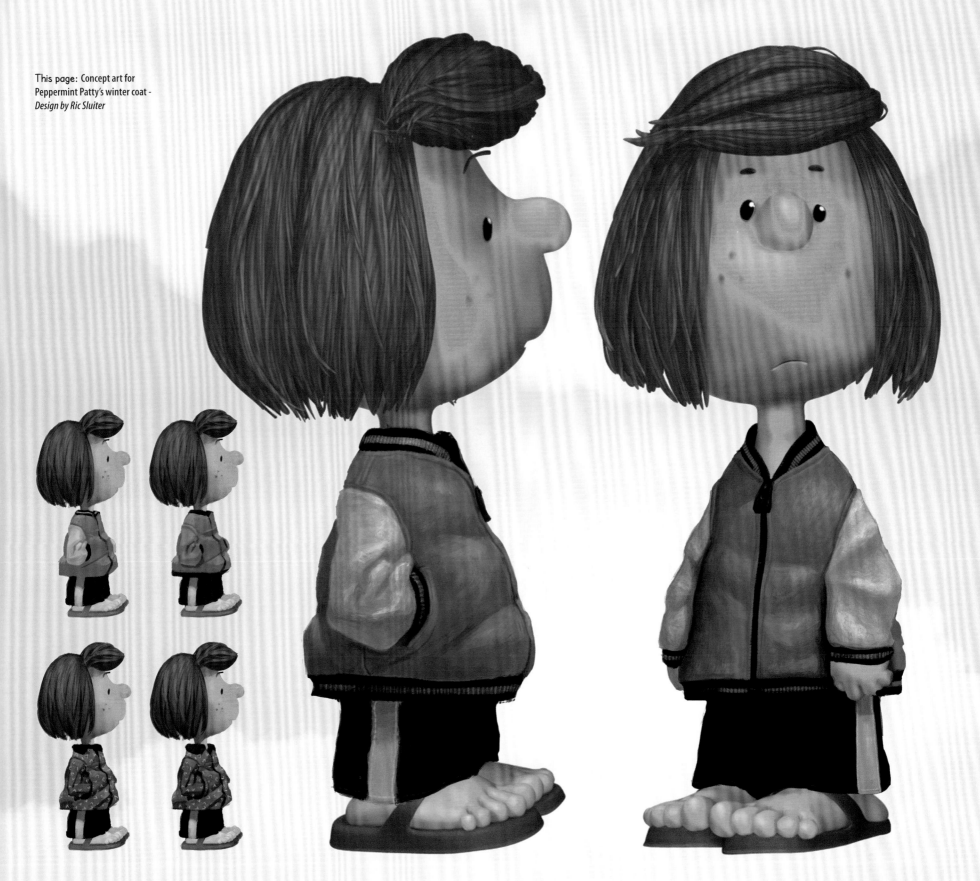

This page: Concept art for Peppermint Patty's winter coat - *Design by Ric Sluiter*

PIGPEN

> I HAVE AFFIXED TO ME THE DIRT
> AND DUST OF COUNTLESS AGES...
> WHO AM I TO DISTURB HISTORY.

Charlie Brown's third baseman Pigpen made his first appearance in the strip on July 13, 1954. He is surrounded by an ever-present cloud of dust wherever he goes, but that is just fine with him, as dirt "likes" him and he views his dust as a badge of honor.

"We could have created realistic dust, with lots of tiny little particles, but we chose to keep the graphic styling that Sparky created in his pen line," says Martino. "When you look at the dust we've created, it is rendered in a similar way that you would in 2D, but unmistakably has the shape language of the strip."

Right: Pigpen - *Final Digital Art*

Above: Concept art for Pigpen's dirt hatch marks - *Design by Baaron Schulte*

Creating Pigpen's trademark cloud fell to the effects team, led by effects supervisor Elvira Pinkhas. Because the characters were being animated on cycles of twos, or twelve frames per second versus twenty-four, figuring out how to create an effect that would stay in sync with the animation presented a unique set of challenges.

"It took us a long time to figure out how to render his dust cloud in 3D," recalls Pinkhas. "We see a lot of him and we wanted to make sure we could translate what we saw in the strip and in the specials into 3D and make sure it would fit the rest of the style of the film."

Through the course of research and developing the effects, the team realized that since the dust is constantly moving and traveling with Pigpen, the cloud and all its particles were merely an extension of the character's movement. "We realized that something needed to travel with the character to serve as a guide for us to create the effects," Pinkhas continues. So for reference, the animators created a half-sphere-like shape that encircled Pigpen, providing a visual cue, approximating space, and expanding and contracting based on the character's actions.

Above: Concept art for Pigpen's dirt hatch marks - *Design by Baaron Schulte*

FRONT INDOOR   PROFILE INDOOR   PROFILE OUTDOOR   FRONT SILHOUETTE   SIDE SILHOUETTE   NEUTRAL   SMILE

Above: Pigpen 'Sparky hero' - *Analysis by Jason Sadler*

Above: Effects components for Pigpen's dust cloud - *Animation by Bert Chung*
Right: Final combined dirt effect Pigpen leaves behind at skating pond - *Animation by Bert Chung*

Above: Pigpen 'Sparky hero' - *Analysis by Nash Dunnigan*
Below: Pigpen dances with Patty - *Final Digital Art*

Above: Concept art for Pigpen's dust cloud - *Design by Robert MacKenzie*
Right: Pigpen skating - *Final Digital Art*
Below: Peanuts, November 16, 1984

"We decided to develop a rig for the dust cloud, which is somewhat unusual for an effects team to handle," says Pinkhas. Senior effects technical director Ilan Gabai created a skirt-based volumetic rig with animation controls that would basically allow all the simulated particles to follow Pigpen wherever he traveled and increase or decrease in size as dictated by the action in the scene.

Turning to the strip for reference, the effects team next set out to create the 3D components that would comprise the actual "dust" of Pigpen's cloud. To differentiate the various details of the dust itself, the effects team identified four components: dust filler, arch outlines, arch highlights and specs. "We looked at the dots that Sparky drew, which weren't perfectly shaped," notes Pinkhas. "Ilan [Gabai] molded the specs in 3D to resemble little pebbles."

Each of the components were independent of each other, giving various other departments, such as lighting, the ability to engage each cloud, arch and dust spec separately.

Above: Pigpen and Lucy are pulled on the ice by Snoopy - *Final Digital Art*

FRANKLIN

Franklin is Charlie Brown's quiet friend and confidant. He made his first appearance in the July 31, 1968 strip, when he befriended Charlie Brown on the beach during vacation. He later became a neighbor and classmate of Peppermint Patty.

As with all the secondary characters in the movie, director Steve Martino wanted to make sure Franklin had a role in the plot. We see him in various capacities, acting as the announcer at the school dance, the emcee for the talent show and making school announcements at assemblies, in addition to being Charlie Brown's friend. "He is kind of like a student council president," Martino says.

In researching the strip for details on the look of Franklin, the artists noticed that his shoes varied from the other characters'. "All the other guys had a rather ordinary looking brown shoe," says Vincent Nguyen, who as the film's lead color designer actually painted the character. "We decided to make the stripe yellow, giving his shoes a sportier look."

Below: Franklin visits Charlie Brown's neighborhood for the first time in Peanuts, October 18, 1968

| FRONT INDOOR | PROFILE INDOOR | PROFILE OUTDOOR | FRONT INDOOR | PROFILE INDOOR | PROFILE OUTDOOR | FRONT NEUTRAL | FRONT SMILE |

Above: Franklin 'Sparky hero' pose analysis - *Design by Jason Sadler*
Right: Franklin - *Final Digital Art*

Above: Concept art for Franklin - *Design by Vince Nguyen*

Above: Concept art for Franklin in winter coat - *Design and Color by Dan Seddon*

Stitching ref

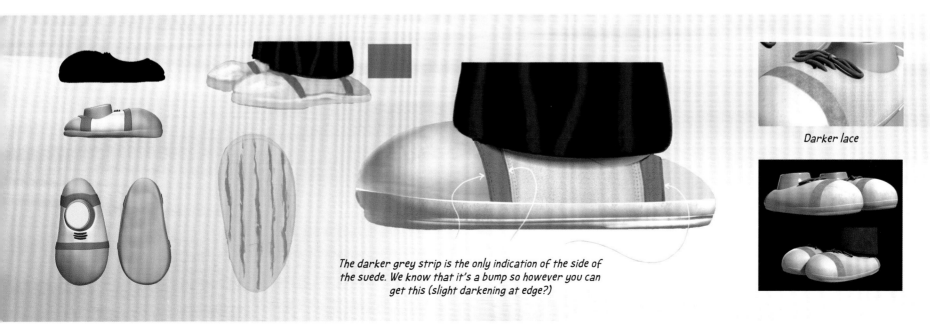

Darker lace

The darker grey strip is the only indication of the side of
the suede. We know that it's a bump so however you can
get this (slight darkening at edge?)

Above: Concept art for Franklin's shoes - *Design by Ric Sluiter*

MARCIE

Peppermint Patty's best friend Marcie made her first appearance in the July 20, 1971 strip. Probably the most logical and smartest of the kids, Marcie provides the much-needed voice of reason in Peppermint Patty's world. What makes the two characters work so well together as a team is that they are polar opposites. Says Steve Martino, "Where Marcie is less of an athlete, Peppermint Patty excels in sports; and while Peppermint Patty struggles with her academics, Marcie is there to act as her tutor."

Just as Charlie Brown has his signature zigzag on his sweater, so Marcie has her trademark glasses. Hiding behind her thick lenses are a pair of eyes that usually stay hidden. In fact, during her entire tenure in the comic strip, Marcie is rarely seen without her trademark glasses.

"When I was asked to paint Marcie, we had to come up with an excuse as to why we do not see her eyes," recalls lead color designer Vincent Nguyen. "We pulled all kinds of reference on thick lenses and aviator glasses and tried various combinations to get the design just right."

Below: Marcie's first appearance in Peanuts, July 20, 1971

Above: A rare glimpse of Marcie's eyes in Peanuts, May 25, 1980
Opposite: Marcie - *Final Digital Art*

Hiding her eyes also meant the animators couldn't use 6s, 9s or periwinkles to convey her emotions. They had to rely on Marcie's glasses to do the job instead. "Since there was a rig built into her glasses, we had the ability to shape the lenses to convey subtle beats of emotion," says supervising animator Nick Bruno. "We were able to hide the fact that we are altering the shape of her glasses by masking change in the movement of her head," adds supervising animator Scott Carroll.

By moving the glasses up or down to indicate excitement or very slightly altering the shape to look like a teardrop to convey sadness, the animators were able to create a significant amount of emotion. "Her performance is pretty amazing," Nguyen acknowledges.

Above: Charlie Brown scores a goal on Marcie at the pond - *Final Digital Art*

Above: Concept art for Marcie - *Design by Vincent Nguyen*

Above: Marcie makes an announcement at the all-school assembly - *Final Digital Art*

FRIEDA

Frieda and her mane of hair made their first appearance in the March 6, 1961 comic strip. Though more proud than vain, Frieda never missed an opportunity to extol the virtues of her naturally curly hair, even when playing center field on Charlie Brown's baseball team.

Although a prominent character early on in the strip's run, Frieda is perhaps best known for her appearance in *A Charlie Brown Christmas*, where not only was her hair "naturally curly," it was bright red. But that presented a problem for the movie.

"The red of Frieda's hair in the reference from the strip and specials was too close to the hair color of the Little Red-Haired Girl," notes lead color designer Vincent Nguyen. "Since the color of the Little Red-Haired Girl's hair defines her character, and the curls define Frieda's, we had to tone down the color of Frieda's hair so that it wouldn't compete with the Little Red-Haired Girl's." After much exploration, the crew settled on a darkish brown/blonde color for Frieda's locks.

Because of her curls, Frieda has one of the most dynamic and complex profiles to manage. Each of her curls, all forty-seven of them, have their own individual rig. To make it look like the curls are actually coming from her scalp, they were attached to little cinnamon roll-like shapes positioned across her head. When she moves, the rolls give her hair a natural movement and bounce.

Right: Freida - *Final Digital Art*
Below: Frieda's first appearance in Peanuts, March 6, 1961

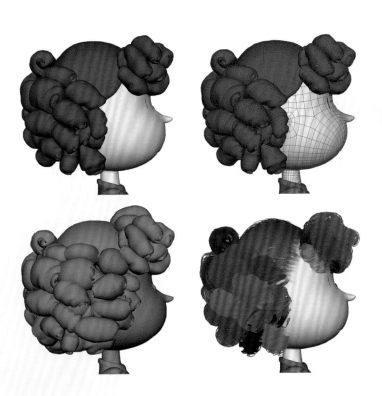

Above: Frieda hair - *Model, Mesh and Fur Model by Adam McMahon*

Above: Frieda - *Final Digital Art*

"We couldn't have a film without Frieda and her naturally curly hair!"

— Steve Martino, Director

Above: Frieda color callout - *by Ric Sluiter*

VIOLET, PATTY AND SHERMY

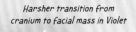

More facial mass

Hair bun is Violet's only distinguishing characteristic in profile

Above: Lucy and Violet analysis - Design by Jason Sadler

The characters of Violet, Patty and Shermy hold a rather unique and illustrious place in the history of Peanuts. They are considered "legacy characters" by many, having made their debuts very early in the strip's run. Patty and Shermy appeared in the very first strip on October 2, 1950, alongside Charlie Brown, and Violet Gray shortly after, on February 7, 1951.

Integrating their characters into the story was important to Martino, but it was just as important for the filmmakers to make sure they weren't lost in the shuffle.

Left: Patty and Violet - *by Charles Schulz*
Right: Violet and Patty's last appearance together in Peanuts, April 17, 1995

"I've always had my favorites, but when I watch Patty and the animation from Blue Sky, the way the animators have developed her own personality just by the way she moves, I fell in love with her all over again."

— Craig Schulz, Writer/Producer

"As we worked on those characters, Patty and Violet in particular, we needed to give them an individual perspective on the story," says Martino. "We came up with the idea to have them be the arbiters of what's 'in' and what's not; the cool kids at school."

For writer/producer Craig Schulz, the way Blue Sky handled the characters offered some insight into his dad's approach. "It's amazing that you can be drawn to characters that you were not really drawn to before," he says. "When you see them in CG animation and the way they interact, you want to know more about Violet and Patty. I can see why my dad loved playing in their world every day."

Above left: Patty 'Sparky hero' poses - *Assembled by Jason Sadler*
Above right: Patty digital sculpt - *Model by Shaun Cusick*

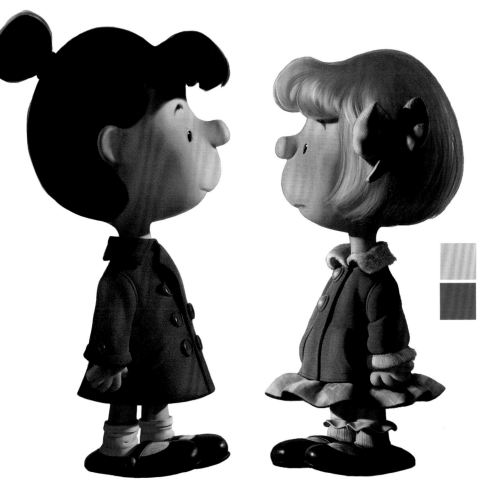

Above: Concept art for Violet and Patty - *Design by José Manuel Fernández Oli*

Above: Animation pose planning for Violet and Patty with Charlie Brown - *Thumbnails and Animation by Lisa Allen, Final Digital Art*

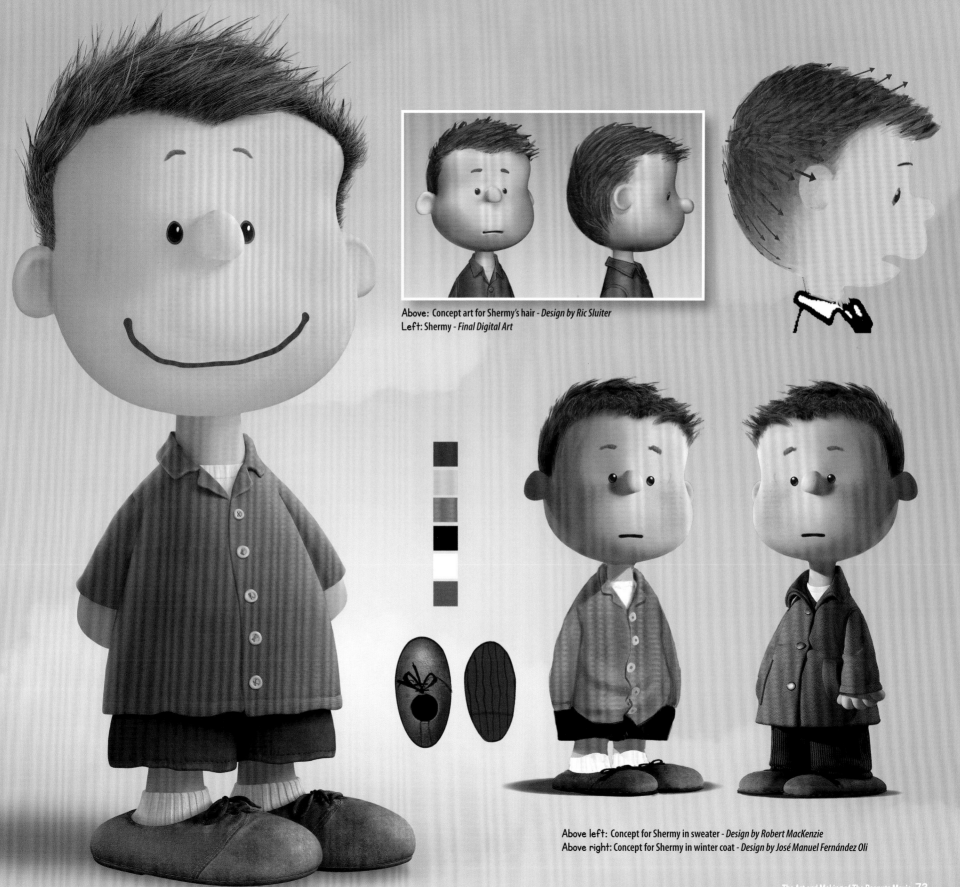

Above: Concept art for Shermy's hair - *Design by Ric Sluiter*
Left: Shermy - *Final Digital Art*

Above left: Concept for Shermy in sweater - *Design by Robert MacKenzie*
Above right: Concept for Shermy in winter coat - *Design by José Manuel Fernández Oli*

THE LITTLE RED-HAIRED GIRL

HAVE YOU EVER HAD THAT FEELING WHEN YOU CAN'T STOP SMILING? YOUR HEART POUNDS INSIDE YOUR CHEST? YOU TRY TO STAND BUT YOUR KNEES BECOME WEAK. AND THEN THAT LITTLE RED-HAIRED GIRL GLANCES AT YOU AND ALL OF LIFE'S POSSIBILITIES BECOME SO CLEAR. AND THEN YOU REALIZE... SHE HAS NO IDEA YOU'RE ALIVE.

CHARLIE BROWN

Combine the coyness of Marilyn Monroe, the mystery of the Mona Lisa and the ability that Helen of Troy possessed to launch a thousand ships and just maybe you might come close to the effect that a little girl with red hair has on our hero, Charlie Brown.

Charlie Brown was first seen pining away for "that little girl with the red hair" in a Sunday strip that ran on November 19, 1961, yet it was not until a daily strip in 1963, nearly two years later, that Schulz introduced the phrase "Little Red-Haired Girl," thus beginning a fifty-plus-year romance.

Although Charlie Brown finally meets the Little Red-Haired Girl in the 1977 TV special *It's Your First Kiss, Charlie Brown*, she is never seen clearly in the strip, only appearing once in silhouette in 1998. That lack of reference from the strip proved challenging for the crew at Blue Sky, as it was important to have the character feel like she was lifted from the strip, just like all the other characters.

"We decided to base the structure of her face on Frieda's face," says character designer Sang Jun Lee. "Since that design, with the more pointy nose, was not

Left: The Little Red-Haired Girl - *Final Digital Art*

Above: The Little Red-Haired Girl walking in the snow - *Design by Greg Couch*
Left: Concept art for the Little Red-Haired Girl silhouette - *Design by Robert MacKenzie*
Right: The only Peanuts image of the Little Red-Haired Girl, May 25, 1998
Below: Concept art for the Little Red-Haired Girl's hair - *Design by Robert MacKenzie*

"DAISY AND GATSBY DANCED.. I REMEMBER HIS GRACEFUL CONSERVATIVE FOX TROT"

used for too many characters, it felt new, but at the same time like she belonged in the world of Peanuts."

To keep the suspense of what the Little Red-Haired Girl looks like building throughout the film, obstacles are thrown in her way, or she passes through crowds, always hiding her face, yet graceful in her movements. So, to convey her personality, the animation team turned to her trademark locks of red hair, with Robert MacKenzie serving as color key artist for the character. Supervising animator Nick Bruno sums up in one word how to convey the Little Red-Haired Girl's personality: "Bounce."

The task of putting the bounce into the character's locks fell to character animator Lisa Allen. While studying what little reference there was available from the TV specials, Allen noticed subtle differences in the way the Little Red-Haired Girl had been animated when compared to the other characters.

"I really wanted to capture that grace and beauty, and everything magical that's wrapped up in Charlie Brown's idea of her," explains Allen. "She does these really slow eye blinks, where her eyelashes flutter and overlap, and she moves a little more slowly than the other characters. I decided to try and see if I could get away with animating her a little more fluidly and gracefully, like those few shots Bill Melendez animated in the Valentine's special. I found that a good way to animate the Little Red-Haired Girl, to both stay true to the animation style of the movie but still have that grace, was to make her hair really flow and move."

Allen's animating skills were put to the test in a scene where Charlie Brown spots the Little Red-Haired Girl dancing in front of her living room window. "It is a really sweet and magical moment," says Allen. "I brainstormed with Nick [Bruno] and Scott [Carroll] and we talked about the ice scene in *Edward Scissorhands*, which had that otherworldly feeling that we wanted to convey."

"[The Little Red-Haired Girl's] personality really came through in that scene in how she moves and sways with ballerina-like movement," observes Bruno. "You can see why Charlie Brown falls for her."

Above: Charlie Brown hides in the potted plant - *Design by Steve Martino*
Right: Color keys - *by Vince Nguyen*
Far right: Charlie Brown hides in the potted plant - *Design and Color by Ric Sluiter*

WOODSTOCK

Snoopy's faithful sidekick Woodstock made his first appearance in the April 4, 1967 strip. Whether the story finds him serving as Snoopy's critical story editor or chief mechanic for his battles with the Red Baron, Woodstock is a loyal friend through it all.

Director Steve Martino compares the dynamic between Snoopy and Woodstock to that of another great duo, Laurel and Hardy. "They share the same simple premise," he notes. "For example, in a typical Laurel and Hardy comedy, all they might have to do is accomplish one simple task: move a piano. But the humor they mine out of twenty minutes of nothing but pantomime is sheer genius and that is exactly the dynamic between Snoopy and Woodstock."

Right: Woodstock's line of action study - *Design by Sang Jun Lee*

Far right: Woodstock - *Final Digital Art*

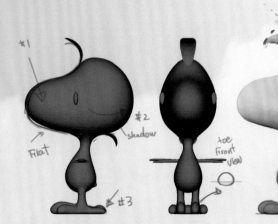

Side View

Overall	✓	✓	✓	✓	✓		
Beak	✓	✓					
Hair	✓					✓	✓
Eyes		✓					

3q View

Overall	✓	✓	✓	✓			
Beak		✓	✓	✓	✓		
Hair			✓				✓
Eyes	✓				✓		

Side View Body

Overall	✓	✓	✓	✓	✓	
Hair			✓			✓
Eyes	✓			✓		
Feet size	✓				✓	
Tail				✓		
Body	✓					

Overall							
Hair	✓	✓					
Eyes			✓				
Feet size			✓				
Tail				✓	✓	✓	✓
Body							

Above: Woodstock 'Sparky hero' pose - *Analysis by Sang Jun Lee*
Right: Woodstock progression - *Model by Adam McMahon*

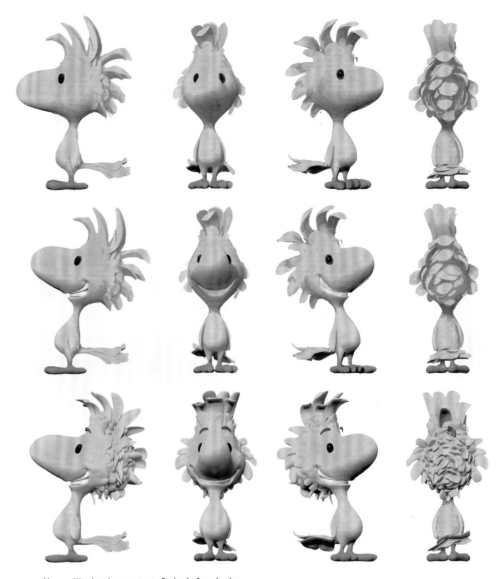

Above: Woodstock concept art - *Design by Sang Jun Lee*

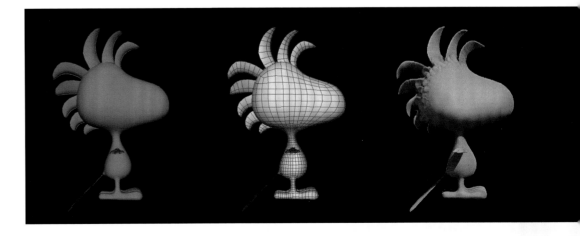

Above: Woodstock and the beagle scouts at the aerodrome - *Final Digital Art*
Left: Woodstock progression - *Model by Adam McMahon*

Behind Woodstock's friendly smile lies a complicated bird. Who knew that such a tiny little yellow creature would present lighting supervisor Jeeyun Sung Chisholm with her biggest challenge? "Woodstock was, without a doubt, one of the hardest characters to light," she says. Because different hues of color in a surrounding environment could easily contaminate a bright canary-yellow color, Chisholm had to be very precise. "If we light Woodstock with cool lights in the sky, he quickly turns green, if we light him with warm lights, he quickly turns orange," she explains. Her team was constantly monitoring all the sequences during final lighting to ensure his color was never off model.

Above: Woodstock is left behind at the toolbox - *Final Digital Art*

"Everyone knows that Woodstock is not the best flyer, but making him do loop-de-loops without making him look like a super-confident, tricky flyer was difficult. I ended up thinking of those loops as little accidents that he falls into, then rights himself and keeps flying."
— **Michael Berardini,** Character Animator

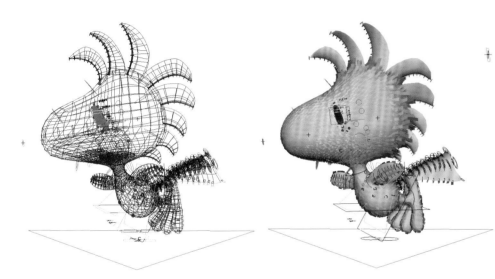

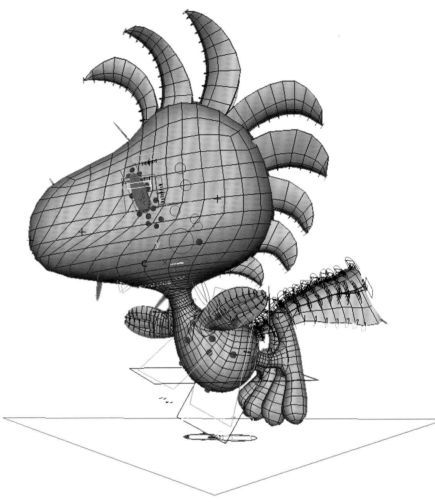

Above: Woodstock's rig and mesh - *Rigged by Brian Anderson, Developed by Steven Song and Adam McMahon*

Woodstock's complexities were not limited to the lighting team. "Translating Woodstock's ambiguous crest of feathers was a huge challenge for our department, probably one of the more difficult ones we faced on this film," admits fur supervisor Jon Campbell. "The eight simple dashes that comprise Woodstock's feathers arching back and over his head are deceptively simple in design."

For Woodstock, the team paid particular attention to the shaping of his feathers and more importantly, how they were placed. The feathers were each rigged, designed to accentuate Woodstock's various expressions and emotions. "He was definitely a lot of work for a little bird," says Martino.

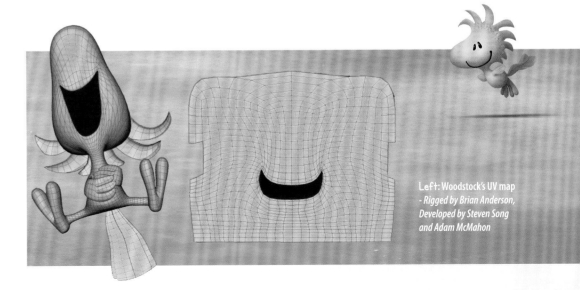

Left: Woodstock's UV map - *Rigged by Brian Anderson, Developed by Steven Song and Adam McMahon*

SPIKE, OLAF, MARBLES, ANDY, BELLE

Named after Charles Schulz's dog from childhood, Spike – with his trademark fedora hat – made his first appearance on August 13, 1975, the first of Snoopy's siblings to join the strip. In the years that followed, Schulz introduced four other siblings to the Peanuts gang: brothers Olaf, Andy and Marbles, and sister Belle.

Spike, Marbles, Andy and Belle share the same basic modeling and rigging design as Snoopy, but when the time came to model and animate

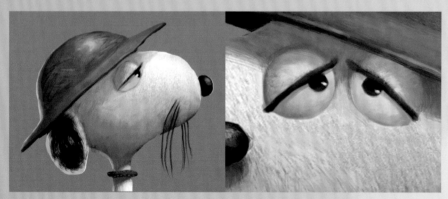

Above: Concept art for Spike's eyes and helmet - *Design by Robert MacKenzie*

Left: Andy, Olaf and Spike appear in Peanuts, June 12, 1997
Right: Spike in fedora - *Final Digital Art*

Above: Concept art for Olaf - *Design by Robert MacKenzie*

Olaf, the artists thought a bit outside the box with regard to his movement.

"Olaf is basically a giant snowball," says supervising animator Nick Bruno. "We made the decision to not give him legs, just two feet moving with rapid-fire energy, which made him a lot of fun to animate."

Left: Olaf - *Final Digital Art*

Above: Concept art for Marbles and Andy - *Design by Robert MacKenzie*
Above right: Concept art for Belle - *Design by Sang Jun Lee*
Below: Marbles visits Snoopy in Peanuts, October 8, 1982

Above Left: Andy, Spike, Snoopy and Olaf enjoy lunch together in bed as Snoopy recovers from a bout of pneumonia in Peanuts, February 22, 1994
Above Right: Belle's first appearance in Peanuts, June 28, 1976

Right: Belle - *Final Digital Art*

AND INTRODUCING...
FIFI!

One other Peanuts dog also appears in the movie: Fifi. Because the look of Spike and Snoopy's other siblings were already well established by Schulz through the strip, designing Fifi presented the filmmakers with a new challenge and an opportunity. "She is seen in a few [TV] specials, but as a quadruped dog, and that is not the direction we wanted to take in the movie," says Bruno.

"Fifi is a photojournalist-pilot documenting the action as she fearlessly flies her trusty Sopwith Camel," explains character animator Lauren Baker. "She knows she has an incredibly important job to do, yet she still finds time for a spontaneous loop-de-loop with the Flying Ace!"

When the time came to design the character, the artists played up the poodle aspect of Fifi with subtle poofs of hair. Explains Scott Carroll, "Fifi needed to look like she belonged in Snoopy's fantasy world just enough, but not resemble one of his siblings, as well as match him in personality."

"It was important for us to not portray her as a damsel in distress," stresses Baker. "We wanted her to be strong, brave and independent, yet in the story, Snoopy does have to rescue her, so it was a fine line to walk."

Left: Fifi - *Final Digital Art*

pointy nose - like Frieda and all the pretty girls

nose bit like Snoopy's

She's a little shorter than Snoopy, but not by much.

similar, but more pronounced concave nose as Snoopy

Sally bangs and ears like Frieda's hair.

skirt fluff

This option, the fluff acts like a fur stole around her shoulders.

tummy and body like Snoopy's

Smaller paws, feet and legs, but essentially Snoopy

least amount of fluff that still says "poodle"

biting poodle.

Above: Concept art for Fifi - *Design by Vicki Scott*
Left: Concept art for Fifi - *Design by Nick Bruno*

Above: Concept art and paintover for Fifi - *Design by Sang Jun Lee, Model by Adam McMahon*

Every photojournalist needs a good camera. But in keeping with the era, Fifi's camera stays true to the World War I period, which meant her camera was slightly larger that those we see today. "My kids barely know what a real camera looks like," jokes Bruno. "When we see Fifi in the sky, pressing a device that looks like a big box, we had to make sure flashes went off and that she motioned to Snoopy with a pantomime smile so that little kids wouldn't think she was shooting at him!"

Left: Concept for Fifi's camera - *Design by Kevin Yang, Color by Ron Defelice*
Right: Fifi and Snoopy - *Final Digital Art*
Below: Fifi painting in Paris - *Design and Color by Tyler Carter*

EXPLORING CAMERA

Cheat to the Camera, Snoopy!

Charlie - Sparky Hero Poses

| FRONT INDOOR | PROFILE INDOOR | FRONT OUTDOOR | PROFILE OUTDOOR | PROFILE PAJAMAS | FRONT INDOOR | PROFILE INDOOR | FRONT OUTDOOR | PROFILE OUTDOOR | FRONT NEUTRAL | FRONT SMILE |

Above: Charlie Brown 'Sparky hero' pose analysis - *Design by Jason Sadler*

Keeping characters on model while in motion is critical to the overall look of the film. Just like every other department, director Steve Martino challenged his camera department to look to the strip for reference. While one might wonder at first why the team would not look to the television specials, cinematographer Renato Falcão and head of camera and staging (also known as "layout") Rob Cardone took to the task and were, as Cardone says, "enlightened" by the amount of information found in the strips.

"Basically, we asked ourselves, 'What would Sparky do if he had a camera when he was drawing the strip? How would he shoot this,'" says Cardone.

For answers, they turned to the strips with a laser-focus on how the character positions changed from panel to panel, how Schulz changed angles and character views to progress the story, and how space was used to give the illusion of movement.

"He might have perspective in the backgrounds, but never the characters' faces," observes Cardone, "relying on the classic poses, or as we call them, 'Sparky View.'"

"Sparky View" is the term that Martino and the crew coined after reviewing thousands of character poses from the strip. "The classic Sparky View pose is the front, full-on view of the character, which is really about seven degrees off center to either side and favoring one ear over the other," explains Martino. "All total, there is Sparky right, Spark left, right profile, left profile, the head totally up in the air, and then on the rare occasion, the tilt-down pose."

Adds Falcão, "Each character is always posed in one of their classic positions, so for us, the challenge was shooting a 3D movie in 3D space, shooting characters with that volume."

"We are using three-dimensional characters in a three-dimensional space and shooting them with a virtual camera with lenses that could potentially change their appearance," continues Cardone. "The audience is so in tune and familiar with these characters in Schulz's two-dimensional comic strip presentation that it was extremely challenging to find the right recipe of lens choice, camera placement and character position within the space to keep them on model and capture the correct proportions and appearance the world knows so well."

To illustrate their observations, Cardone and Falcão offer an in-depth analysis of a few key strips and panels that provided a basis for the camera work and staging.

"A perfect example of what Renato observed about character poses," explains Cardone. "She is probably not really looking at him at all, and he's not looking at her. So in conversational sequences where we would normally cut to an over-the-shoulder shot, we instead need one character in a three-quarter Sparky View, and the other character in profile, to emulate the stip. In this case the eye lines will definitely not line up because the characters are not actually looking anywhere near each other. This is one of the many spatial challenges that would be immediately exposed in stereo."

"Dynamic camera angles were not something [Schulz] did very often," says Cardone of this early strip of Charlie Brown and Lucy. "You can see that he was trying to work out his style." To reinforce the notion that Schulz was evolving his perspective on the strip, Cardone references a Charles Schulz quote from the fiftieth anniversary book *Peanuts: A Golden Celebration*:

"Why aren't there any grownups in Peanuts? Well, there just isn't room for them. They'd have to bend over to fit in the panels.

"The answer isn't really a joke, as this is the only strip where you see the grass from a side view... If you added adults, you'd have to back off and it would change the whole perspective."

"You really can't suggest an adult in any way," says Cardone. To prove that point, the crew did experiment with a shot during the classroom sequence. "We tried a shot of the teacher [the never seen and cleverly heard Ms Othmar] entering the classroom and seeing the kids," recalls Cardone. "From an adult perspective the camera was above the characters' eye level looking down. It really felt out of place. The kids looked tiny. It looked weird!"

"This strip shows us a great example of an implied tracking shot," says Cardone. "Between the Schulz character poses and the panel compositions in the ice, you really get the sense that a camera is following Snoopy's every move."

LINUS AND SCHROEDER WILL BE WINGS..

JANUARY 23, 1972

In this strip from 1972, the characters of Schroeder and Linus are looking down, the tops of their heads somewhat visible. "That was something Schulz rarely did, so this particular panel proved extremely insightful for the rare occasions our camera movement called for this type of action," notes Cardone.

PEANUTS

April 16, 1961

"You can almost see the animation and flow in the size of the panels and as Lucy's emotion changes," notes Cardone. "There is a pacing to this strip from panel to panel, starting flat, then adding some depth for the impact moment, and finally back to flat."

SOMETIMES I LIE AWAKE AT NIGHT, AND I ASK, "WHY AM I HERE?"

THEN A VOICE SAYS, "WHERE ARE YOU?"

"HERE," I SAY... "WHERE IS 'HERE'?" SAYS THE VOICE..

"WAVE YOUR HAND SO I CAN SEE YOU"

THE NIGHTS ARE GETTING LONGER..

© 1993 United Feature Syndicate, Inc.

APRIL 24, 1993

"The way the panel size narrows during Charlie Brown's dialogue in this strip from 1993 to me suggests a camera drifting in. I thought that was fascinating. It's hard to believe Schulz wasn't thinking about that [camera movement]," says Cardone.

In the mid/late 80s Schulz started to experiment with difference sizes of panels, including single-panel strips for the daily comics. "They really are like paintings," observes Falcão of the single-panel strips.

To Falcão and Cardone's amazement (and ultimately the entire crew), upon closer examination of the single-panel strips, they realized that when a 1:85 aspect ration frame scaled to the size of the strip was applied to the panel and moved from left to right, a "two panel" story was revealed, or in other words, a setup and payoff. Cardone cites four strips as classic examples of Schulz's use of a 1:85 aspect ratio applied to the panels.

"They are all perfectly composed"
— Rob Cardone, Head of Camera and Staging

In these panels from two Sunday strips, May 22, 1955 and March 24, 1963, Cardone was particularly intrigued by the amount of depth and high camera angles in the panels from 1955 compared to the panels from 1963. "You see that nearly ten years later Schulz had established a flatter style of how he staged the strip," he explains. "The two strips pretty much contain the same type of action of a character attempting to catch the fly ball, but in the latter years, the flat staging of the character action and eye-level camera placement is basically the Peanuts style we all know and love."

ANIMATION
You're Going to Van Pelt University, Snoopy!

To lead the team of animators that would be responsible for the crucial task of bringing the characters to life, director Steve Martino turned to three of Blue Sky's seasoned artists: supervising animators Nick Bruno and Scott Carroll, and lead animator Jeff Gabor. All three were brought on early in the process and are ardent fans of Charles Schulz. "We wedged ourselves onto this project," jokes Carroll.

When Blue Sky Studios and Twentieth Century Fox Animation announced in 2012 that the company would be producing a CG film based on Peanuts, Bruno sums up the general consensus of the animation studio in one word, "Crazy!" Adding, "We knew instantly the challenges we were going to face from day one, so we set out to one hundred percent honor the comic." Gabor concurs: "Everybody who came on board the project wanted to get it right."

The trio was responsible for training, supervising and most importantly, keeping on model a team of one hundred animators. Stressing clarity, focus and simplicity, Bruno, Carroll and Gabor had to introduce an animation style that was new to nearly everyone working on the film. Each new animator joining the team would attend "Van Pelt University," a crash-course in the study of Charles Schulz's style and work.

Although the animators certainly pored over the thousands of comic strips for reference on the look of the characters, when the time came to explore basic movements, the strip, while a great visual reference, was lacking in movement cues for the animators.

"There was not a whole lot of information to go on from the strips for movement," observes Gabor. "When you start to break down Snoopy's fifteen or twenty expressions, it was impossible to decipher the in betweens for movement cues, so we turned to the specials."

The specials are, of course, the television specials produced by Bill Melendez and Lee Mendelson. Over the course of thirty-eight years, starting in 1965, the duo produced forty-five television specials, winning three Emmy awards and an additional twenty nominations. As well as winning an Emmy, the first, *A Charlie Brown Christmas*, also won a prestigious Peabody Award. In 2015, the program celebrates its fiftieth anniversary, and to many Americans, the airing of the special signals the official start of the Holiday Season.

Very early on in production, animation development lead BJ Crawford created a pencil test and decided to use Peppermint Patty as his subject. "When I came onto the project the animation reference we had to work with was from the Peanuts specials. Since we all agreed that we had to embrace the charm and feel of that work, we decided

on an approach that became incredibly useful to us."

Relying on the classic Peanuts comic strips for poses, gestures and acting choices, such as how she would hold the phone, Crawford then turned to the specials for movement cues. "These were the qualities that I tried to place in the original pencil test of Peppermint Patty," says Crawford. "I think it really helped to convince the creative team that we could develop a look that was unique in contemporary animated film, but also stay true to the original material."

Working closely with lead character designer Sang Jun Lee and art director Nash Dunnigan, the animators were already well versed in Sparky View and discovered that Melendez had faced similar challenges when he first attempted to animate the characters. In fact, in a 2005 interview, Bill Melendez recalled his first experience with translating the characters from the script to the small screen:

"I had to animate Sparky's characters in such a way that you wouldn't see the turns. I found ways of animating this and hiding the fact that [the] scope of the movement was very limited. Snoopy saved me, because Snoopy is more like a real animated character. He can do anything – move and dance – and he's very easy to animate, whereas the kids are nearly impossible! I've always had to think quickly and learn how to cope with the limitations of the design."

"If you look at what Bill Melendez did, it is like you are still looking at the strip," observes Carroll. "The style he created for the specials was in large part due to the design of the characters."

"I listened to hours and hours of taped interviews with Bill [Melendez] from the later part of his life and he learned that you can't animate these characters in a follow-through fashion," adds Martino. "The in between images looked terrible and that knowledge is what drove his styling."

It would be remiss to mention the work of Melendez and Mendelson without a nod to the work of legendary animator Bill Littlejohn, responsible for animating two of the most memorable scenes of Peanuts animation: Snoopy's enthusiastic dance on top of Schroeder's piano in

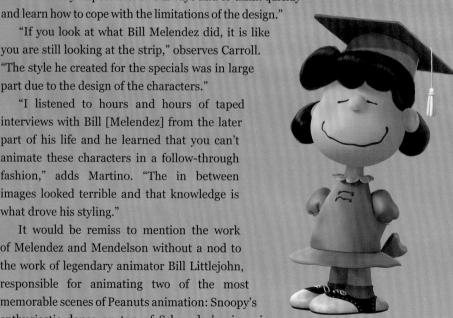

Above: Lucy - *Final Digital Art*

Above: 2D animation test of Peppermint Patty on the phone with Charlie Brown - *Animation by BJ Crawford*
Left: *Peanuts*, October 17, 1980

A *Charlie Brown Christmas* and the visually graphic animation of the Red Baron sequence in *It's the Great Pumpkin, Charlie Brown*. His ability to translate Snoopy's antics and pantomime into story has been lauded and studied by aspiring animators all over the world, including those at Blue Sky.

"Bill Littlejohn gave me my very first understanding of animation," recalls Bruno. "When I was five years old, I received a Cartoon Viewer for Christmas, that came complete with a set of Peanuts animation. I would stay up all night stepping through Bill Littlejohn's masterpiece [sequence], Snoopy vs. the Red Baron. There was something magical about fully understanding that Snoopy was on the losing end of a dogfight without ever seeing his opponent!"

"Most CG character rigs are based off of a model that works from all angles, a character based off of anatomy," explains Carroll. "So if the Peanuts characters needed a different, modeled pose for each specific angle, we had to find a way to make the rig

highly flexible, yet very specific to what we needed. Many technical problems ensued, but if we hadn't studied Bill Littlejohn's work, I'm sure we wouldn't have gotten that iconic Peanuts look and feel to the animation."

Achieving the extreme trademark character poses and iconic expressions of Snoopy – that Melendez and Littlejohn were able to produce in traditional 2D with relative ease – provided its own unique set of challenges for Gabor, who as lead animator also served as the co-lead on Snoopy along with Joe Antonuccio.

"Snoopy is completely different," explains Gabor. "The kids' heads stay round in every scene, so that one rig works. Although Snoopy can smile and have the same range the kids have in their smiles, he also has to open his mouth, in particular when he laughs at the Red Baron, which requires additional controls in the rig that allows him to open his mouth in exaggerated and extreme poses."

To achieve the desired simplicity of the characters, as well as continuity, the

Above: Snoopy progression: model, mesh and rough fur - *Model by Adam McMahon*

supervisors told the animation team to do away with their usual cheats and shortcuts and even approach to basic pacing and movement. Nearly every animator will tell you that they will actually "act out" a scene they are working on in front of a mirror or record their own performance for reference to aid in the choreography of a scene. In a departure from that technique, the team at Blue Sky was instructed to do the exact opposite. "We told everyone to think through the choices in their head," explains Bruno. "There's something more organic about *thinking* through the acting choices versus acting them out. What you miss out on in the physicality, you gain in simplicity, which is inherently more Peanuts-like." Carroll agrees. "The limitations foster new creativity, new solutions and new acting choices."

Keeping the characters on model would of course be crucial to the process, so to aid all the animators, the supervisors created a Peanuts Movie Style Guide to serve as a checks and balances throughout production. Everything from guidelines on height, poses and shape language was included in the manual. The team even developed a clever way to convey the various iconic shapes of the characters' arms, feet and hands – with food! Loaves of bread for the shoes, eggs to depict the soles of the feet and drumsticks to convey the forearms were just a few of the references the team identified.

In the early days of the exploration phase, the animation team would refer to poses from the strips and attempt to move the characters in CG in a more traditional way, animating at 24 frames per second (or "ones"). But as suspected, that approach led to less than impressive results. "We realized that when you [animate] in a more traditional way, the nose, eyes and ears literally change position and it makes the character look like it's, well, melting," says Bruno.

To achieve the desired transitions between poses, for example from a front view to side view, the team decided to animate at 12 frames per second ("twos"), which resulted in a much snappier, cleaner final look. "Animating on twos also works well with the graphic quality of the characters and the simplicity of the strip itself, giving the film a stop-motion feel," says Carroll. "We got the whole studio to buy into doing the film at a lower frame rate and stay true to the comic strip," adds Gabor.

The decision to animate on twos (and sometimes even threes) was not without consequences, resulting in a ripple effect throughout the production pipeline.

"We had to actually animate clothing instead of simulating it," explains Carroll. "Because we were holding [animating] on twos, the computer was unable to mathematically calculate the smooth simulation of clothes." When animating at 24 frames per second there is fluidity in the movement from frame to frame, allowing the cloth simulation to follow a character's movements seamlessly. The start-and-stop nature of animating at 12 frames per second would have resulted in the clothes vibrating and falling off the characters!

The animators also realized a second good reason to animate the clothing. When a typical cloth simulation was applied to the characters, the clothing would simply drape on the body underneath, as the animators would expect. But in the case of the Peanuts characters, "The silhouette is key," continues Carroll. "It is what defines the characters and even the slightest deviation away from their iconic silhouettes takes them off model."

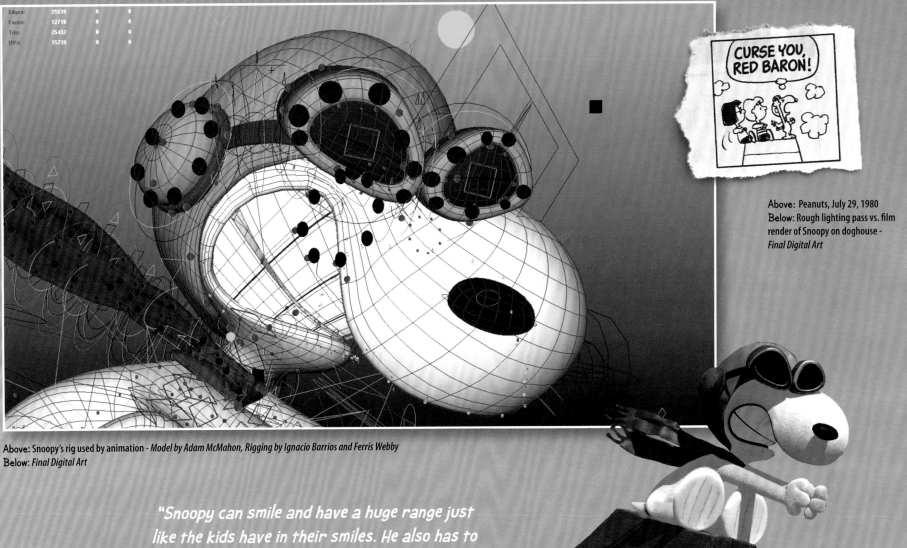

Edges:	25539	0	0
Faces:	12716	0	0
Tris:	25432	0	0
UVs:	15739	0	0

Above: Peanuts, July 29, 1980
Below: Rough lighting pass vs. film render of Snoopy on doghouse - *Final Digital Art*

Above: Snoopy's rig used by animation - *Model by Adam McMahon, Rigging by Ignacio Barrios and Ferris Webby*
Below: *Final Digital Art*

"Snoopy can smile and have a huge range just like the kids have in their smiles. He also has to open his mouth very wide when he 'curses' and laughs at the Red Baron, which meant we needed another rigging control that had to be built into his overall rig. We then had to figure out a way to build the shape of his mouth and develop the range of motion for those moments."

— **Jeff Gabor,** Lead Animator

It's Your Imagination, Charlie Brown!

Above and Right: Charlie Brown's imagination sequence 2D animation - *by BJ Crawford*

In the film, there are a few key moments when we enter the imagination of Charlie Brown. The sequences – including when Charlie Brown imagines a clean slate with the arrival of a new neighbor, winning the school dance competition and a first kiss with the Little Red-Haired Girl – are clear standouts in the film. To differentiate the look of Charlie Brown's thoughts from that of the rest of the film, director Steve Martino turned to animation development lead BJ Crawford to animate the sequences. "I wanted those moments to look as close to the black and white comic strip as possible, authentic to Sparky's pen and ink line, but fully animated," says Martino.

"The challenge was to determine what style was best for the project," explains Crawford. "My thought was that if the characters would be hand-drawn, their line quality and design should be as close to the Schulz artwork as possible. I did some initial tests that used the correct shape and weight of Schulz's line and to my relief it seemed to work with everyone who saw it.

"I think the most important factor in creating the 2D sequences for *The Peanuts Movie* is the investment of time," continues Crawford. "It's a look that requires you to focus on every frame of animation as if it were a single drawing from the original strips. The drawings are entirely informed by Schulz's own line work. My approach is to plan and research as much of the scene as I can before I even approach the animation itself. That means poring over countless strips in search of the right poses and gestures that will fit the emotional needs of the scene. I then take a pass at storyboarding the scene using as much composition language and ideas from the strips as possible. I animate the scene digitally using software that still allows me to draw every frame of artwork. Once the motion of the characters is correct, I use that as a guide to go in and create a new 'inked' drawing for every frame of film."

To accentuate the "flicker effect" seen behind the animation, Crawford used scans of actual Bristol illustration boards similar to the boards used by Schulz when drawing the strip. "We photographed the boards at different times to give the illusion of seeing five sheets of paper going by you, which is what creates the flicker effect."

Martino was especially pleased with Crawford's results. "BJ's work in these sequences is the best interpretation of Schulz's line," praises the director.

"This project for me was an incredible honor to work on," says Crawford. "It really pushed me as an artist. I love embracing another artist's style; it always ends up being harder than you'd initially think it might be. You really have to approach the work in a humble and entirely new way without falling back on solutions to problems that you'd normally default to."

You're Not Seeing Double, Charlie Brown, They're Just Your Ghost Limbs!

Once the decision was made to animate on twos and sometimes threes, it became clear that the use of motion blur to bridge the gaps between fast movements over varying degrees of distance was not going to be an option for the animation team. "To compensate, we developed a method to selectively utilize parts of a fully rigged character," explains character development supervisor Sabine Heller. The technique, dubbed "ghost limbs" by the artists, enabled the animators to effectively cheat using multiple rigged arms, hands, feet and legs to accomplish what was done in traditional 2D animation, where an animator would draw a frame to suggest motion blur.

"Peanuts characters have a very unique anatomy. They don't have real elbows, finger joints or shoulders. They don't have knees either."

— Paige Braddock, Creative Director, Charles M. Schulz Associates

Above: *Final Digital Art*

Above: Hand analysis - *by Nick Bruno and Scott Carroll*

ENVIRONMENTS
Happiness is a Colorful World

Left: Charlie Brown and Snoopy in the living room - *Color Key by Robert MacKenzie*
Above: A comparison showing the simplified shapes and flatter staging of Peanuts in later years for Charlie Brown's living room, March 27, 1960 (left) and May 9, 1989 (right)

Translating the film to the big screen in CG was a daunting task, and not just for the animators. Creating the overall look of the film was just as challenging for the art department. "I always looked at the comic strip and wanted to know a little more about Charlie Brown's world. I wanted to look around the corner of the comic strip panel and see what was there," says Martino. "[Schulz] always just gave us a short snapshot, a tight shot of their world."

Although the TV specials offered a broader look into the world of Peanuts, the focus was squarely on the characters rather than their surroundings. "I never got a sense of the rooms or a consistency of rooms, where the house was, how big it was or where it 'lived' in the neighborhood in relation to everything else," observes Martino.

Expanding the world fell to art director Nash Dunnigan and his team.

"Sparky is, in essence, our production designer for the film," says Dunnigan. "His original comic strips provided a wealth of information for our visual approach." Spending countless hours poring over comic strips, the design team worked to figure out the common threads weaved throughout the panels. It was important to Dunnigan to not only maintain a consistency in design, but to not over-embellish the film either. "You can only take the level of detail in the props and environments so far before there's a disconnect," he explains. "We didn't want to push the production value so high that it would compete with the intended simplicity of the characters' and the film's look."

One of the more charming aspects of the strip is that the characters seem timeless. "We tried to achieve timeless styling in order to avoid dating the film – with a few exceptions," explains Dunnigan. "We tried to stay away from concepts that were not in Sparky's strips." While populating the background of Charlie Brown's living room, the design team explored including a television as a prop. In researching the strips, the team had noted that some featured a 1970s console-type television set. "We designed and modeled the TV," recalls Nash, "but decided not to use it as we felt it dated the scene and film. It introduced multi-media and a 'decade' and we didn't want to introduce those concepts." One exception the filmmakers made was the iconic rotary phone seen in so many of Schulz's strips and comics.

With characters whose wardrobes represent every major color in the crayon box, lead color designer Vincent Nguyen was faced with a unique challenge when the time came to develop the color script of the film. "Usually, characters will dictate the look of the backgrounds," explains Nguyen. "Since the signature colors of the characters were pretty much predetermined, we had to work to slightly dial-down the background colors to allow the cast to come forward, so they weren't competing for your attention."

While the strip provided ample reference for the character design phase, it was slightly more difficult to pick up on color cues. Fortunately, Dunnigan and Nguyen were able to turn to the book *Peanuts Jubilee: My Life and Art with Charlie Brown and Others* by Charles M. Schulz. Published in 1975 to celebrate the twenty-fifth anniversary of Peanuts, the large-format book features full-page reproductions of Sunday strips in full-color. "Schulz himself selected the background colors when they printed the book, so we were able to cue off a lot of flat color references," says Nguyen.

Above: Flying Ace interrupting Charlie Brown and Linus at the thinking wall - *Color by Vincent Nguyen*

Right: One of the wall's many appearances in Peanuts, January 4, 1992

"We found that 50s and 60s colors tended to be more neutral and worked better for the film, whereas the 90s tended to be more saturated."

"Although the information in the strip is more illustrative in the 50s and 60s, with more detail in the props and line, it was actually less helpful because [Schulz's] whole aesthetic evolved over the years. The shapes of the objects became simplified and he staged things much flatter in later years," says Dunnigan of why the Blue Sky team decided to use design reference from the 80s and 90s, yet look to the earlier years of the strip for background color palette cues for the movie. "Tom Everhart said that when he studied [Schulz's] work, all the superfluous stuff was taken out as he progressed into the 70s, 80s and 90s. It was all about character and dialogue. The set design just crept in every now and then, serving to support the story. There was a charm in the way he drew the strip in the 80s, and like the characters, the set design evolved over the years. We decided to use that cartoony, simplistic graphic shorthand for the environments."

Dunnigan (and Martino) urged the design team and artists to constantly refer back to the pen line of Schulz's work in everything they designed. But in looking at the span of strips from the 80s and 90s, as Schulz's backgrounds, set dressing and props

(for lack of better terms) acquired a much more simplistic aesthetic, the artists were left to fill in a lot of blanks. "We would review the strips and only see part of a lamp or couch, just a corner of a window," recalls lead set designer Jon Townley. "It became even more important to absorb the nuances of how [Schulz] drew and his style."

With a narrative structure that finds Snoopy taking off on flights of imagination as the World War I Flying Ace, developing the movie's look had a second layer of complexity. Director Steve Martino knew he wanted to draw a clear distinction in the production design between the action that takes place in the beagle's fantasy sequences and those that take place in the "real world." Knowing that the scenes taking place in Charlie Brown's house, in the school and throughout the neighborhood would all be styled with more desaturated background colors, it made sense to push the color palette for Snoopy's flights of fancy. "We wanted to explore a lot of contrast between the imagination of Snoopy's fantasy and the real world of Charlie Brown," says Nguyen. With Snoopy primarily white, the deeper colors of the spectrum would only serve to accentuate his actions.

The design team subsequently ended up settling on two distinct looks for the film: "Charlie Brown World" and "Snoopy's Fantasy World."

CHARLIE BROWN WORLD

Meet You at the Ice Pond, Charlie Brown!

Above: The skating pond - *Final Digital Art*

Replicating the background design of Schulz's strip proved to be a lesson in minimalistic design for lead set designer Jon Townley and his team of artists. Using the strips from the 80s and 90s as a guide, Townley soon discovered that half the battle would be filling in an enormous amount of blanks. "In the thousands of strips we reviewed, [Schulz] would only draw part of a window or tree, so we basically had to look to the left, right, up and down and imagine the rest of the space in the round," says Townley.

To fill in those blanks, Townley turned to the subtle lines and shapes of Schulz's pen line. "When you look closely at the rhythm of the shapes and the way they flatten out, start and stop, and go from thick to thin all in one line, we basically extrapolated the line to create full profiles for all the trees and background elements."

Everything from trees to clouds and snow was interpreted by the design team, and all share the unique shape language and rhythm of Schulz's line.

"Jon culled through all the reference and found iconic samples of small twiggy branches with really subtle gestures," recalls art director Nash Dunnigan, "which provided a template on how to translate those pen strokes into an entire tree." Townley even created an entire design scheme for the grass and ground, based on the "little sprigs here and there" that Schulz would hint at in the strip.

Using photo reference from scouting trips of Schulz's hometown in Minnesota, combined with reference from the strip, the filmmakers populated the background primarily with spruce, maple, aspen and birch trees. The most prominent tree in the film – and the most notorious tree in the entire Peanuts universe and Charlie Brown's nemesis – the kite-eating tree, is a maple tree.

"Aesthetically the film was definitely challenging for us," acknowledges materials supervisor Brian Hill, who worked on *Epic* and *Rio 2*, both of which were hyper-realistic, stylized worlds. "Both films required an enormous amount of detail on all the

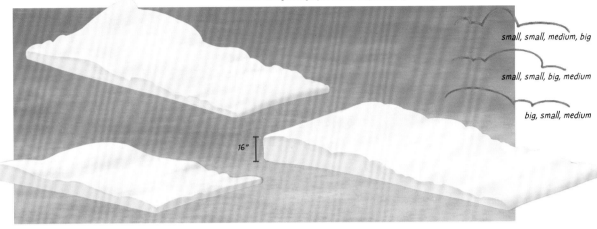

Sparky used a very lyrical line to express snow, notice how no two "loops" are alike, always varying in width, height and symmetry

small, small, medium, big

small, small, big, medium

big, small, medium

16"

Above: Concept art for snow styling - *Design by Tyler Carter*

Above: The Kite-Eating Tree makes another appearance in Peanuts, March 4, 1990

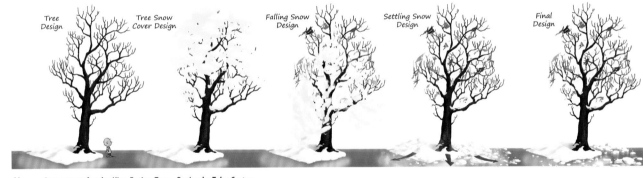

Tree Design

Tree Snow Cover Design

Falling Snow Design

Settling Snow Design

Final Design

Above: Concept art for the Kite-Eating Tree - *Design by Tyler Carter*

"Steve wanted us to feel always as if we might be looking at the Sunday comic strip when we were in Charlie Brown's world."
— **Nash Dunnigan**, Art Director

Above: Concept art for small tree variations - *Design by Jon Townley*

surfaces," says Hill. "Translate that to the world of Peanuts, though, and too much detail looks very off model and out of place. We had to work closely with the design team and the director to make sure we struck the right balance in detailing all the surfaces and textures."

If you look closely at the strip, whenever Schulz would fill in large spaces, such as tree trunks, Snoopy's ear, Lucy's hair or the sides of houses, quick pen strokes and line would fill in the space, sometimes leaving white space. Dubbed "Sparky Fill" by the crew, the same approach was applied to the film. "So the detail that we do put into the environments are key elements that give it enough sense of what that specific surface is, but are not too realistic," adds Hill.

The placement and staging of all the trees and environmental elements fell to the assembly team, led by Gareth Porter. "Our primary goal is to make sure that none of the set dressing distracts from or conflicts with the action," says Porter. "For example, when Charlie Brown is on the pitching mound, we make sure that from all camera angles, there isn't a tree branch in the background sticking out from his head!"

"The biggest global challenge in the set design of the film was having to re-think the simplicity pass," says Townley. Knowing that a realistically styled environment would not work with the aesthetic of the character design, let alone the tone and style of the strip, both the design and assembly teams worked to identify assets that needed to be tweaked or removed so as not to compete with or distract from the action.

A less crowded and complicated environment also proved challenging to the lighting team. "In other films we have worked on, we've populated jungles with hundreds of trees, so if one shade of green is slightly off in the lighting, your eye won't notice, it will simply blend in with the rest of the foliage," explains lighting supervisor Jeeyun Sung Chisholm. "But in this film, since everything is so meticulously placed with specific purpose, if just one tree looks slightly out of balance lighting-wise, you will notice and it will take you out of the moment."

Aspen/Birch reference

Right: Peanuts, August 21, 1994
Below: Concept art for spring-time trees - *Design and Color by Tyler Carter*

Aspen leaf
The veins are patterned after Sparky's line.
The primary vein should have displacement,
while the secondary and tertiary ones should
be much more subtle.

Above, First row: Concept art for the aspen leaf - *Design by Robert MacKenzie*
Above, Second row: Concept art for the maple leaf - *Design by Tyler Carter*

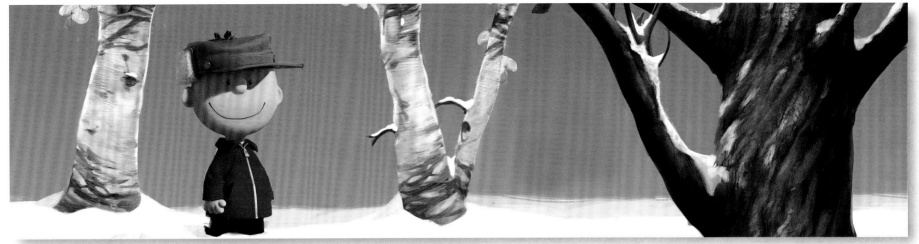

Above: Early concept art for tree bark texture - *Trees by Ric Sluiter, Charlie Brown by José Manuel Fernández Oli*

Maple reference

Right: Peanuts, January 7, 1992

"*The colors in Charlie Brown World should always support the characters. Nothing overly saturated, saving the saturated colors for the characters.*"

— **Nash Dunnigan**, Art Director

The Doctor is In, Charlie Brown!

Despite 65 years of inflation, Lucy still provides sound (sort of), reasonable (not really) and heartfelt (she really does try) advice from her lemonade stand/psychiatric booth at the bargain basement price of 5 cents. And Charlie Brown keeps coming back.

In an early scene of the film, after the arrival of the "new kid" in the neighborhood, Charlie Brown seeks out Lucy's counsel. This scene was also one of the first scenes that cinematographer Renato Falcão and layout supervisor Rob Cardone worked on, testing multiple lens packages to see how far they could push depth of field while at the same time keeping the characters on model. The scene with Charlie Brown and Lucy at her booth and the proximity of the characters in relation to each other provided a great opportunity to explore various lenses. "The challenge was how do we shoot these characters without feeling the depth on these very round characters." Below you can see how the characters appear through various lens sizes. Ultimately, Falcão and Cardone settled on using a range of lenses, between 55mm and 85mm, for the film, with 50mm lenses working for wide, establishing shots, and an 85mm lens for close-ups."

Top right: Color key - by Robert MacKenzie
Right: Lens diagram - by Nash Dunnigan

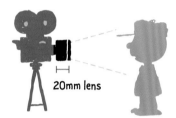

20mm lens

Camera had to be *close* to Charlie Brown

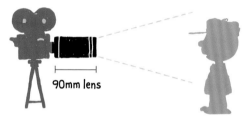

90mm lens

Camera had to be moved *far away* from Charlie Brown

20mm

30mm

40mm

50mm

60mm

70mm

80mm

90mm

Above: Charlie Brown and Lucy at the psychiatric booth, seen through lenses with different focal lengths - *Camera and Staging by Ken Lee, Final by Dan Barlow and Karyn Monschein*

"LET ME LET YOU IN ON A LITTLE
SECRET, CHARLIE BROWN. IF YOU
REALLY WANT TO IMPRESS GIRLS,
YOU NEED TO SHOW THEM
YOU'RE A WINNER!"
LUCY VAN PELT

Above: Color key - *by Robert MacKenzie*
Below: Lucy and Charlie Brown at the psychiatric booth - *Design by Jon Townley, Color by José Manuel Fernández Oli*

For lead material technical director Nikki Tomaino, the scene between Lucy and Charlie Brown at the booth is probably her favorite moment. "The scene at the booth was the very first sequence of the film that went through lighting," she recalls. "It was the first time we got to see it all in context, with the lighting and materials complete. It was really rewarding to be in the room with everyone just looking around in awe of the result of all our hard work."

Above left: Psychiatric booth model without materials - *Model by Krzysztof Fus*
Above right: Concept art for Lucy's psychiatric booth - *Design by Tyler Carter*

Above: Peanuts, September 22, 1963
Below: Animation posing - *Animation by Lisa Allen*
Below middle: Chair and coffee can - *Design by Jon Townley*

Above: Concept art for text on the psychiatric booth signs - *Design by Nash Dunnigan*

Above: CG render of the psychiatric booth set without materials - *Model by Krzysztof Fus and Cleveland Hibbert*

Left and Above: Thumbnails and Animation - *by Lisa Allen*
Below: *Final Digital Art*

Wake Up, Peppermint Patty, Class is In Session!

"We went through a number of looks when deciding on the color for the lockers in the school hallways," says Dunnigan. "With a full palette of primary colors representing the kids, we wanted to make sure we selected a color they would all look good against." After much debate, lead color designer Vincent Nguyen settled on a desaturated shade of dark teal for the lockers.

"Making sure the characters popped off the backgrounds was very important," says Nguyen. "Throughout the school, all the secondary colors of the backgrounds in the hallways, the cafeteria and the walls of the classroom are very muted shades of teal, ochre and brown, and then slightly graded down so that the characters read well, especially our hero cast."

For the color scheme of the auditorium, where the talent show and school assembly take place, Nguyen chose muted shades of maroon, purples, dark reds and browns. "They are colors you would expect to find in your local movie theater, but at the same time maintain a timeless quality to the palette," he adds.

In direct contrast to the muted browns and teals of the hallways and cold, steely environment of the cafeteria set, the classroom palette includes warmer colors to soften the mood a bit.

Great attention was also paid to the set design of the props and desks. Once again "finding the line" in everything from the window shades and the chalkboard, right down to the beveled lines in the desks.

"Rather than fill in entire spaces with solid black ink for the strip, Schulz leaves gaps in the scratches of the fill, but never completely covers the space, which we dubbed 'Sparky Fill.' You would see that a lot in the strip with Lucy's hair or Snoopy's ears. In our sets, we applied that same technique to the sides of a desk or chair."

— **Brian Hill**, Materials Supervisor

Right: Charlie Brown hiding in his desk - *Design by Jon Townley and Color by Vincent Nguyen*

Above: Charlie Brown at the front of the class - *Design and Color by José Manuel Fernández Oli*

Above, left to right: CG model of classroom set with no materials - *Model by Andre Rodriguez and Ramon Lopez;* Concept art for classroom props - *Design by Sandeep Menon, Ric Sluiter and Kevin Yang, Painting by Vincent Nguyen and Ric Sluiter*

Right: Charlie Brown's desk in Peanuts, March 21, 1971, and Peppermint Patty's, October 21, 1990

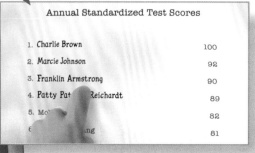

Annual Standardized Test Scores

1.	Charlie Brown	100
2.	Marcie Johnson	92
3.	Franklin Armstrong	90
4.	Patty Pat____Reichardt	89
5.	Mo____	82
6.	____ng	81

Schulz looked to his real-life friends for inspiration when naming the characters. Appearing on the list of test results are a few of those names: Marcie Carlin, Heather Wold (a one-time crush of Schulz's and inspiration for the Little Red-Haired Girl), Shermy Plepler, Patty Swanson ("original" Patty), Frieda Rich and Patricia Reichardt (Peppermint Patty). The name 5 95472 (full name "555 95472") is a nod to Schulz's reaction to the US Post Office issuing zip codes in the 1960s, basically "reducing people to a number." The zip code 95472 is the postal code for Sebastopol, California, where Schulz resided at the time. 5 and twin sisters 3 and 4's claim to fame are their memorable dance moves, first seen in A Charlie Brown Christmas.

For cinematographer Renato Falcão and layout supervisor Rob Cardone, staging and shooting scenes in the classroom proved somewhat of a challenge. "Once we determined that we would be leaning towards shooting with longer lenses, we realized the spaces would need to be very accommodating to shutting off the walls and breaking away sections of furniture so that we could position our camera with a 50mm lens, which is pretty far away from the subject," says Cardone. Offering a comparison to other film mediums, Cardone explains, "In a live-action film, you basically have breakaway walls that are removed so you shoot the objects with the desired lens, but in animation, the walls are modeled, so we simply turn off that section of the model." In addition, because the perspective of the desks from the front of the classroom varies from that of the side, assembly supervisor Gareth Porter and his team would rearrange the classroom based on specific camera lens choices. "When shooting in profile, the desks are spaced normally," explains Porter. "But when shooting from the front they are spaced further apart so that the scene has a sense of depth."

One very important moment occurs in the classroom environment: the entrance of the Little Red-Haired Girl. Director Steve Martino knew the introduction of Charlie Brown's crush had to make an impact, so he turned to lighting supervisor Jeeyun Sung Chisholm. It was important for Martino to keep the suspense building for the big reveal of the Little Red-Haired Girl's face. Her introduction to the kids in the classroom scene is beautifully lit, casting her in silhouette (a nod to her only appearance in the strip).

"As she opens the door and enters the classroom, we added an almost dreamy backlight to promote her mysterious image," says Chisholm. "But even though she is backlit, we paid special attention to make sure you could still read the colors of her hair and dress."

With fifty years worth of characters, stories and fun facts, the filmmakers couldn't resist putting a few "Easter eggs" in the film, many of them hidden right in plain sight throughout the school.

Top: *Final Digital Art*
Above: Color key - *by Ron Defelice*

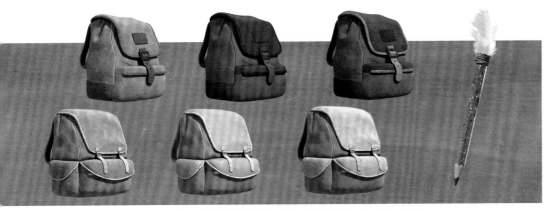

Above: Color palette for backpacks and pencil - *Color by Kevin Yang, Materials by William Liu and Travis Price*

Not only does the case in the hallway contain trophies, it features a hidden gem for even the most diehard Peanuts fan. "If you look closely at the list of names of test results, some of them are friends of my dad and the inspiration for the character's names," says writer/producer Craig Schulz.

"In a nod to Peanuts trivia," adds producer Michael Travers, "Charlie Brown suggests a book that Violet and Patty read for their next book report, titled *Spark Plug*, which is where Schulz's nickname 'Sparky' came from." Spark Plug was a popular character featured in one of Schulz's favorite comic strips, Barney Google by Bill DeBeck.

Above: Color keys - *by Ron Defelice*
Right: The Little Red-Haired Girl arrives - *Design by Tyler Carter*
Bottom right: Lucy is splattered with paint - *Final Digital Art*

"In an homage to Tom Everhart's painting Lucy's Scream, a remote-control tri-plane spirals out of control, flying around the classroom. The plane knocks over a bunch of paint cans, spraying paint all over Lucy's face, matching Tom's style."

— **Steve Martino,** Director

Above: Concept art for moving van - *Design by David Dibble*

There are two main vehicles that are seen in Charlie Brown World. In a nice homage to Emmy award-winning legends Bill Melendez and Lee Mendelson, their surnames provide the name of the moving company's van that arrives in the neighborhood early in act one. "They are responsible for creating and producing timeless animation that defined a generation," says producer Michael Travers. "We always knew we were going to pay homage to them, but it needed to be organic. What better way than to plaster their names on the side of a huge truck!"

The other major vehicle is the anxiety inducing mode of transportation dreaded by Charlie Brown and other like-minded grade schoolers: the school bus. "I remember when I was a kid and taking the bus, the seats were this ugly dark green color," says lead color designer Vincent Nguyen. While not an altogether ugly color, the art department settled on a muted, saturated shade of green/teal for the bus seats. "Charlie Brown's winter coat is red, so we took liberties in tweaking the green to make it a more pleasing color so that it would look good against his coat," adds Nguyen.

"With both vehicles we paid close attention to making sure the lines were not symmetrical and in keeping with Schulz's pen line," says art director Nash Dunnigan. "At first glance you may not notice the windows of the school bus are varied in shape and size, but if they were all the same size, like the real world, you would notice that something is not quite right."

Above: Charlie Brown hiding under the bus seats - *Color Key by Ric Sluiter*

Above: School bus development - *Design by Sandeep Menon, Model by Krzysztof Fus*

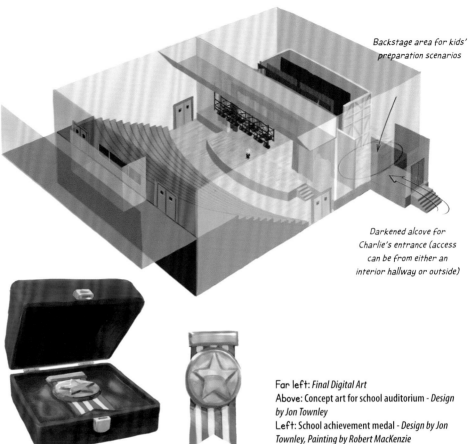

Backstage area for kids' preparation scenarios

Darkened alcove for Charlie's entrance (access can be from either an interior hallway or outside)

Far left: *Final Digital Art*
Above: Concept art for school auditorium - *Design by Jon Townley*
Left: School achievement medal - *Design by Jon Townley, Painting by Robert MacKenzie*

You're a Regular P.T. Barnum, Sally Brown!

Non transparent balloons
opaque balloons

Like a mini P.T. Barnum in pink, Sally Brown knows a good opportunity when she sees it. Capitalizing on her big brother's fleeting fame, Sally embarks on a merchandising scheme, hawking everything from T-shirts and posters to mugs and balloons. In preparation for her big debut, she even gives "tours" of Charlie Brown's bedroom!

When it is revealed during the school assembly that there was an error in calculating test scores, Sally's enterprise comes crashing down around her.

Above: Sally's merchandise booth outside auditorium - *Design by Robert MacKenzie*

This is Your Neighborhood, Charlie Brown!

In designing the interiors of Charlie Brown's house, art director Nash Dunnigan and his team wrestled with balancing the warm skin tones against the warm, softer colors used by Schulz in the strip. "Their heads are such a big orb of yellowish warmth," notes Dunnigan. "We had to make sure that they would not merge into the background with a similar color temperature." Working closely with lead color designer Vincent Nguyen (and input from lighting supervisor Jeeyun Sung Chisholm), they ended up selecting a desaturated lavender shade. "While not your first choice for an interior of a living room," says Nguyen, "the combination really worked."

Above: *Final Digital Art*
Left: Charlie Brown's neighborhood - *Previsualization*
by ShengFang Chen and Jesse Lewis-Evans
Below: *Final Digital Art*

Right: Living room furniture - *Design by Sandeep Menon, Model by Adam McMahon, Eryn Katz and Cleveland Hibbert*
Far right: Living room scale study - *Analysis by Nash Dunnigan*
Below: Concept painting of Charlie Brown's living room - *Design by Sandeep Menon, Color by Vincent Nguyen, Charlie Brown by José Manuel Fernández Oli*

Right: Notre Dame Cathedral in Paris (September 8, 1978). Pen on paper - *by Charles M. Schulz*
Far right: Street scene in Paris, with cars and children playing ball (September 11, 1978). Pen on paper - *by Charles M. Schulz*
Courtesy of the Charles M. Schulz Museum and Research Center, Santa Rosa, California.

Some of the paintings hanging on the walls of Charlie Brown's house are reproductions of non-Peanuts works by Charles Schulz.

For the interior of the Little Red-Haired Girl's house, seen from Charlie Brown's point of view from the outside looking in, the lavender shades were bumped up a bit brighter, along with soft pinks and other pastel colors, all to accentuate and draw attention to her signature red hair.

Since the characters are mainly small kids, scale also presented a few conundrums to the design team. "We didn't want the Peanuts characters to feel like toddlers," says Dunnigan. "We allowed for some exaggeration in the scale of the props, but all the while keeping in mind that the scale of the objects in relation to Charlie Brown and all the characters should be relatable to what we know and feel is natural, not toy-like in their proportions."

The design team also had to develop a consistent look for the buildings in Charlie Brown World, one that would be relative to all the characters. "That was nearly a two-week discussion," recalls Dunnigan. "In the strip, [Schulz] would sometimes show the kids being able to reach the doorknobs, and sometimes they couldn't. We settled on what made the most sense for Charlie Brown's height, so we standardized the sets based on that."

When the time came to design the various bedrooms of the gang, Dunnigan designed the initial color schemes of each room, cueing off each character's primary focal color – blue for Lucy, red for Linus, purple for Schroeder and so on – as well as their personality for set dressing. "Schroeder is obviously into music, so you see a bust of Beethoven next to his bed," observes Nguyen. "And he's a bit more mature, so the color scheme of the room reflects that in the muted olive tones."

The team had a lot of fun designing the various posters, sports pennants and other props to populate each room, even throwing in an inside reference in Charlie Brown's bedroom. "We put a model plane in Charlie Brown's bedroom that is a replica of a World War II P-40 plane that Craig Schulz restored and has in his hangar in Santa Rosa," says

Above: *Final Digital Art*
Left: Charlie Brown's WWII P-40 toy model - *Design by Ramon Lopez, Color by Nash Dunnigan*
Below: Color keys - *by Kevin Yang*

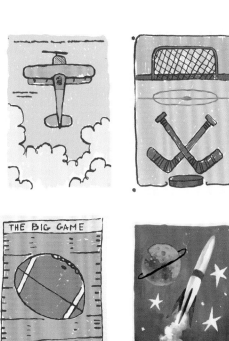

"I think my favorite set is Charlie Brown's bedroom at night. It really reminds me of my own room as a kid; the same colors, the posters, even the one little lamp that illuminates the whole room. Seeing Charlie Brown sitting at his desk doing his homework really resonated with me. When you're at that age you're kind of hiding in your room."

— **Nick Bruno,** Supervising Animator

This page: Concept art for Charlie Brown's bedroom posters and pennants - *Design by David Dibble and Kevin Yang*

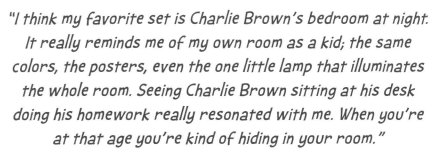

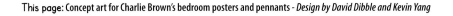

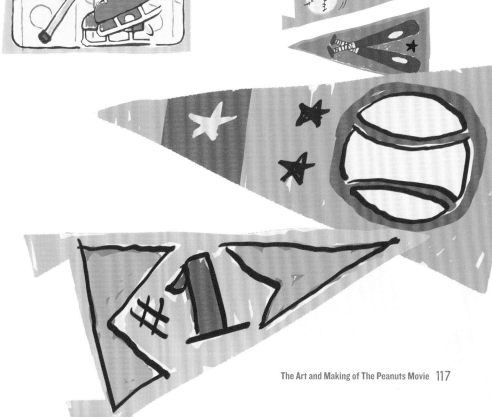

Above: *Final Digital Art*
Right: Charlie Brown's house - *Design by Sandeep Menon, Color by Nash Dunnigan*

Martino. "It really does go a long way in enhancing the story," adds assembly supervisor Gareth Porter, whose team basically acts as set decorators (as their live-action counterparts are known) by placing all the items and props in a scene. "Not only does it tell you a lot about the character, it helps you to stay in the moment with the story."

The exterior of the houses proved, once again, to be a case study in the pen line of Schulz's style.

Above: Charlie Brown's house in Peanuts, October 31, 1982
Right: Lucy's garden in Peanuts, June 3, 1990

"I did an entire case study on how much wiggle and bevel is seen on each of the panels, and the difference in how the lines translate in close-ups versus far away shots," says lead set designer Jon Townley.

Knowing that when viewed on a large canvas not only perception but depth would be a key factor, Townley paid close attention to the details when it came to construction and design of the sets. "In all of our architectural and mechanical objects, we focused on controlling the edges and profile shapes, while at the same time being mindful to never pull focus from the characters."

Above: Concept color studies of background neighborhood houses - *Design by Jon Townley, Color by Vincent Nguyen*

Above: Renders of Charlie Brown's house and the Little Red-Haired Girl's house - *Design by Sandeep Menon and Jon Townley, Models by Cleveland Hibbert*

Above: Color key - *by Ron DeFelice*

Far right: Charlie Brown knocked off the baseball mound by a line drive - *Design by Jon Townley, Color by Tyler Carter*
Right: Color keys - *by Ric Sluiter*

Below: Peanuts, June 27, 1980

You're In the Spotlight, Charlie Brown!

WHY, WHEN I WIN THAT FIRST PRIZE
RIBBON, THERE WILL BE NO ONE
WHO HASN'T HEARD THE NAME
SALLY BROWN AND HER TRUSTY
HORSE, BROOMSTICK!

SALLY BROWN

Above: Charlie Brown's magic act - *Sketches
by Steve Martino*
Right: Storyboards - *by John Hurst*

The night before the big talent show finds Charlie Brown rehearsing his magic act with Snoopy. It's actually a pretty good act and Charlie Brown feels pretty confident about his chances of taking home the big trophy and impressing the Little Red-Haired Girl. Unfortunately, the evening does not go quite as planned. From the wings, Charlie Brown watches sister Sally's cowgirl act, which starts off well, but to everyone's horror, poor Sally suffers from a case of stage fright. "To put it bluntly, she's bombing," says art director Nash Dunnigan. Thinking on his feet, Charlie Brown does what any good big brother would do, he ditches his magic act, makes an impromptu cow costume, and together with Snoopy, takes the stage and rescues Sally's act.

Above: Color key - *by Robert MacKenzie*
Left: Everyone reacts to Charlie Brown arriving at the talent show - *Final Digital Art*

Creating a cow costume and then animating Charlie Brown, as a cow, was easier said than done. "We went through a lot of design concepts for the cow costume and none were working," recalls Dunnigan, "but then Nick Bruno came up with the idea of riffing on the old-school Halloween outfit from that special." The outfit is, of course, a nod to Charlie Brown's attempt to cut two simple holes in a sheet for his ghost costume. In the original movie, the end result is a multi-holed sheet that looks unassuming but, observes Dunnigan, "When he's on all-fours, it looks like a cow. The animators did a great job at animating it, driving the scene with the physical comedy of Charlie Brown under the sheet."

In yet another clever nod to the specials, in particular the moment in the Christmas special when Lucy is barking orders as the stage manager of the play, while Snoopy stands next to her pantomiming her words, "There is a moment in the film when Lucy is putting doubts into Charlie Brown's head before the talent show starts," explains Dunnigan. "And we see projected on the screen what we think is her image and see her mouth moving. But in reality, it is really Snoopy!"

Left and Below: Concept art for Charlie Brown's costume - *Sketch by Nick Bruno, Design by Ron DeFelice and Kevin Yang, Painting by Vincent Nguyen*

Finger painted quality
black paint

Top: Charlie Brown on stage in his cow costume - *Final Digital Art*
Above: Photos from the talent show - *Final Digital Art*
Right: Sally rides Snoopy in the talent show - *Final Digital Art*

Just Follow the Beagle's Lead, Charlie Brown!

One evening while taking out the recycling, Charlie Brown spots the Little Red-Haired Girl across the street, dancing in her living room. "It's night-time, and she's beautifully lit," says Steve Martino. "A light bulb goes off in his head, and he realizes that she likes to dance."

Charlie Brown runs back inside and immediately starts to practice his dance moves... with a mop. He realizes that if he can learn to dance and win the school contest, then maybe he'll get to dance with her. Less than impressed with Charlie Brown's dance moves, Snoopy takes it upon himself to give a few pointers. As the scene progresses, Charlie Brown drifts off into a daydream where he's dancing with the Little Red-Haired Girl, a sequence animated by BJ Crawford. When he comes back to reality, it's not the Little Red-Haired Girl in his arms, but rather Snoopy!

Head of story Jim Kammerud recalls storyboarding the actual school dance scene that takes place later in the story and the subtle difference storyboard artist Karen Disher added to her boards that informed the animators. "In the dance sequence, Charlie Brown comes through the door with a punch bowl," explains Kammerud. "It's not just that he's stuck in the door with a punch bowl that makes it funny, but rather the look on his face, and that's what Karen brought to that scene to make it work."

Tree and snow dance decorations

Above: Concept for school auditorium - *Design and Color by Tyler Carter*

Above: Winter dance school poster - *Design by Ron DeFelice*

Above: Color key - *by Robert MacKenzie*

SHE'S HERE!

SHIRT STUCK

DANCE

NEED:
1. BIGGER DANCING THAT TAKES CHARLIE BROWN ON A MORE CRAZY PATH
2. KIDS START TO MIMIC ONE OF HIS MOVES

Above: Storyboard panels of Charlie Brown entering the school dance - *Design by Steve Martino*

Below and Right: Color Keys - *by Robert MacKenzie*

In a very typical Charlie Brown moment of failure, he also gets doused with "rain" during the dance sequence, courtesy of the school's sprinkler system.

"When it rains in a standard CG film, we create little balls of water and let motion blur and gravity take over, making it look like they travel downward, taking the shape of a droplet," explains effects supervisor Elvira Pinkhas. "But since the animators are animating on twos and sometimes threes, we don't have that luxury of motion blur in this film." So Pinkhas and the effects team followed a reverse engineering process to figure out how to make the water droplets look like they are elongated and blurry.

"In the specials we found stylized droplets, but while looking through reference from the strip, we noticed all sorts of curves, hooks and irregularity to the pen strokes," says Pinkhas. "We thought it would be great to imitate the actual lines from the comics, so we modeled our own geometry, which was a new challenge for our effects team."

Turning to reference of Schulz's pen line from the strips, the artists, led by effects technical director Doug Seiden, painstakingly created and modeled ten different versions of rain droplets of varying shapes and length that could be stretched and elongated. The "rain droplets" were in turn placed into the frames of the film, appearing as brief flashes. "Every drop of water in the film is a piece of modeled geometry," Pinkhas proudly states.

In a fun twist, towards the end of the scene, the sprinkler system douses Pigpen (*see* page 62), rendering him clean... and unrecognizable to Patty.

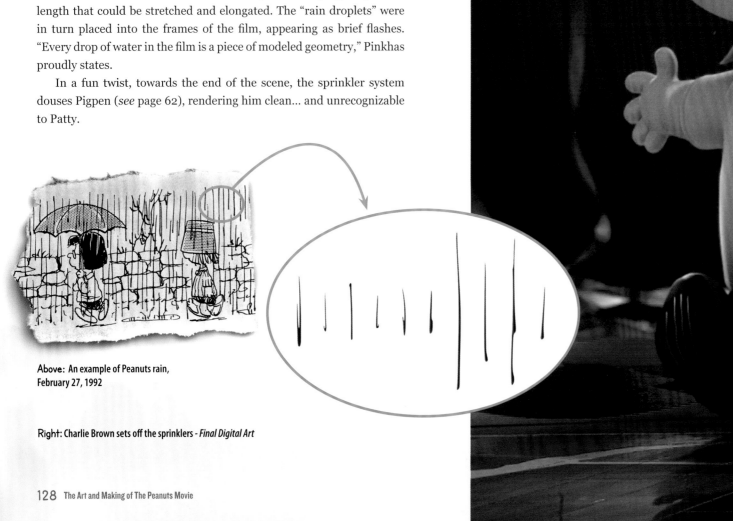

Above: An example of Peanuts rain, February 27, 1992

Right: Charlie Brown sets off the sprinklers - *Final Digital Art*

"One of the things my dad was most proud of was drawing rain. When you think about it, he was working with India ink. You screw one up, you'd have to start the comic strip all over!"
— Craig Schulz, Writer/Producer

Peppermint Patty's No Librarian, Charlie Brown!

Above: Library exterior concept art- *Design by Jon Townley, Color by Ric Sluiter*
Right: Library interior concept art - *Design by Jon Townley*

I JUST MIGHT BE ABLE TO HELP YOU THERE, CHUCK. MARCIE JUST READ OFF A LONG LIST OF GREAT NOVELS. *HUCKLEBERRY SOMETHING, CATCHER WITH A PIE.* BUT SHE SAID THE GREATEST BOOK OF ALL TIME IS CALLED *LEO'S TOY STORE* BY SOME OLD GUY CALLED WARREN... UH... PIECE.

PEPPERMINT PATTY

Just like that, Peppermint Patty sends Charlie Brown off to the library in search of the greatest book of all time, "*Leo's Toy Store* by Warren Piece." Fortunately for Charlie Brown, once in the library, he has the guidance of Marcie to set him on the correct path.

The art department and lighting teams went to great lengths to differentiate the various sections of the library, creating a whimsical and colorful kids section in direct contrast to the adults section where Charlie Brown ultimately finds Marcie and a copy of Leo Tolstoy's *War and Peace*. "Think Harvard versus the local kids library," comments art director Nash Dunnigan on the differences in color and lighting design.

Right: Color keys - *by Ric Sluiter*

  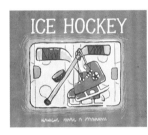  

    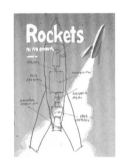 

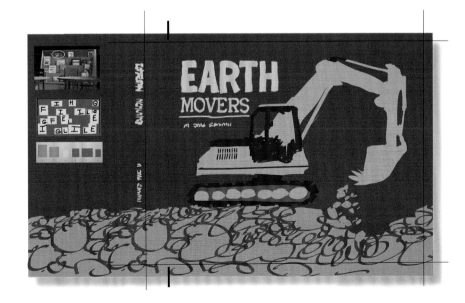

This page: Concept art for children's library books - *Design by Ron DeFelice*

Left and Top: Color keys - *by Ric Sluiter*
Below: Charlie climbs the ladder in the library - *Final Digital Art*

9/23/14

Nick Note: add in looking beat of him looking @ worm for audience to look @ it, too.

Shhhhhh...

Left: Animation sketch pose planning - *Thumbnails by Lauren Baker*
Below: Concept for worm book - *Design by Ron DeFelice*

Back view of pop up elements is one color for worm, and one color for the apple.

Front color treatment on the pop up elements

"There are a lot of really great moments that take place in the library," adds Dunnigan. "One of my favorite scenes in the film is where Snoopy, acting as librarian, keeps 'shushing' Woodstock, who can't control his laughter while reading a pop-up book."

Above: Snoopy warns Woodstock to be quiet in the library - *Final Digital Art*

Follow Your Heart (and Kite), Charlie Brown!

Left and Above: Carnival set - *Design by Jon Townley*

It's the last day of school, and what better way to celebrate than with a big carnival before sending some of the kids off to summer camp. One of the kids attending summer camp is the Little Red-Haired Girl and Charlie Brown is determined to find her in order to have a key question answered, one that he has been pondering for some time. Believe it or not, it is his kite that ultimately leads the way...

"Because it was so important to be able to see and track Charlie Brown during his search for the Little Red-Haired Girl, we knew we had to stay away from the color yellow in the scene," explains lead color artist Vincent Nguyen. "And not just any yellow, but primary cadmium yellow!"

All the carnival booths, prizes and rides intentionally have a flat, muted color design to them, to convey a timeless quality, as if the setting could be "Anytown, USA," in June.

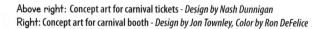

Above right: Concept art for carnival tickets - *Design by Nash Dunnigan*
Right: Concept art for carnival booth - *Design by Jon Townley, Color by Ron DeFelice*

Left and Above: Concept art for carnival fun house - *Design by Jon Townley*

Above and Right: Color keys - *by Ron DeFelice*

Color Your World, Charlie Brown!

"The color script is the first impression of the movie as a whole," explains lead color designer Vincent Nguyen. Using the color script as a guide, the filmmakers are able to get a sense of everything from timing, pacing and most important, the highs and lows the audience may experience while watching the story unfold on the screen. "It serves as an emotional beat board," add Nguyen. "You're able to take a step back and examine where you might be spending too much time, or not enough time, on specific beats, allowing the director to shift color and either dial in or dial back where needed."

This spread: *The Peanuts Movie* color script - Color Lead, Vincent Nguyen

Act 1

Act 2

Charlie Brown World

Snoopy's Fantasy World

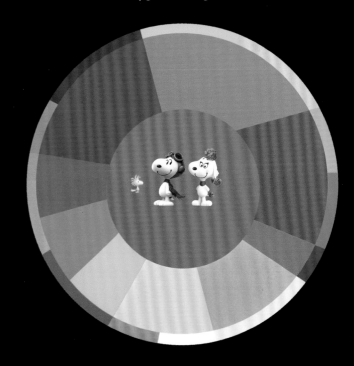

Act 3

SNOOPY'S FANTASY WORLD

In the Snoopy's Fantasy World sequences we find Snoopy as his "World Famous Author" persona, struggling to write the next great novel. With his trusty editor Woodstock by his side, the two of course bicker over the direction of the story.

For the writers, this was an especially fun narrative structure, given that the action takes place in Snoopy's imagination. "We see the story progress as Snoopy takes cues from what he sees going on in Charlie Brown's life," says writer/producer Cornelius Uliano. Of course the most recent twist in Charlie Brown's life is the arrival of the Little Red-Haired Girl, which informs the plot of Snoopy's novel.

"Snoopy's story is filled with love and adventure," continues Uliano, "set against the backdrop of World War I as the Flying Ace sets off to win the heart of a beautiful pilot named Fifi, while facing off against his arch-nemesis, the Red Baron."

The "chapters" of Snoopy's novel – narrated in voice-over by Lucy in the film – set up each sequence, and Snoopy's latest classic, *The Greatest Story Ever Told*, opens with Snoopy's trademark first line.

Below: Snoopy pursues the Red Baron over countryside - *Design by Tyler Carter*

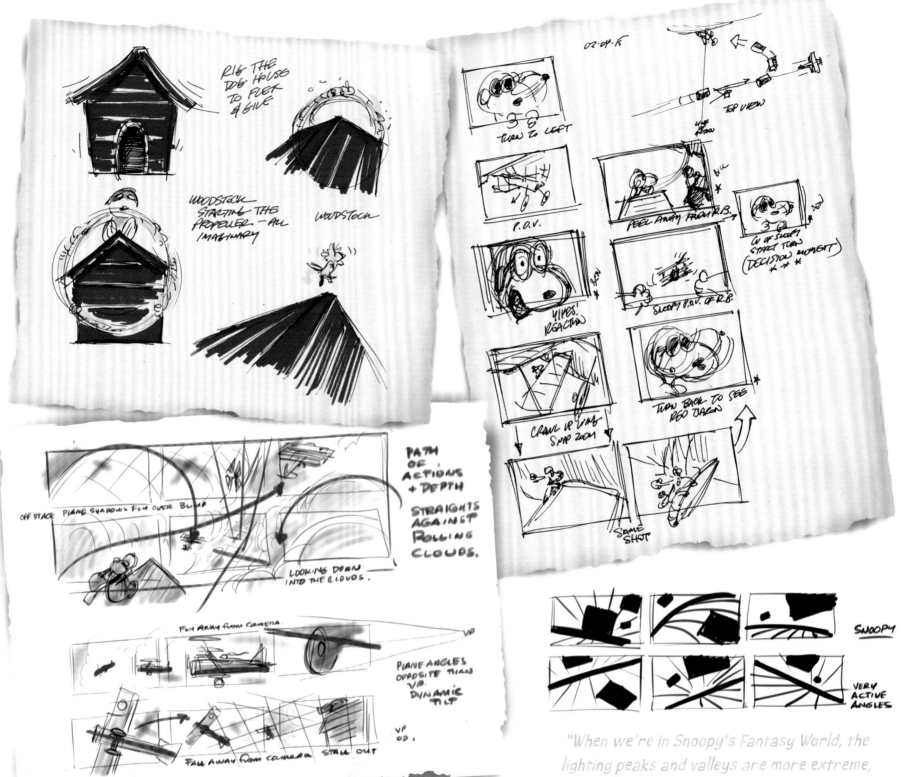

Above: Concept storyboard drawings - *Designs by William H. Frake III and Steve Martino*

"When we're in Snoopy's Fantasy World, the lighting peaks and valleys are more extreme, enhancing the emotion through color."
— Vincent Nguyen, Lead Color Designer

It Was a Dark and Stormy Night...

Above: 'Dark and stormy' sequence - *Camera and Staging by Harald Kraut, Final by Gene Kim*

In direct contrast to Charlie Brown World, where the characters never come out towards the audience, the rules in Snoopy's Fantasy World are much more flexible. "In Snoopy's imagination, we can utilize the depth of space so that it feels like we've taken a trip to a different place," says Martino. "We still need to maintain Sparky View poses for Snoopy, which means no three-sixty shots around Snoopy, but when we are flying, the sky is the limit!"

There is, however, one minor limitation in Snoopy's Fantasy World. In the strip, it was important for Schulz to convey a sense of fantasy, which is also crucial to the film. Therefore, to lend credibility to the piloting skills of the World War I Flying Ace and stay in the moment inside Snoopy's imagination, the bottom of Snoopy's doghouse is never seen. "Sparky never showed it in the strip," observes Martino. "He always cropped the base of it so our imagination would fill in the rest – that he's flying." With that one stipulation, cinematographer Renato Falcão and layout supervisor Rob Cardone took to the challenge, creating exhilarating and dynamic camera angles for the sequences.

"When you go into Snoopy's Fantasy World, it has to be just mind-blowing, which is exactly what Steve did, starting with a fantastic opening sequence."
— **Craig Schulz**, Writer/Producer

Right: Color key - *by David Dibble*

Above: 2D and 3D animation pose and camera planning for 'dark and stormy' sequence - *by Jeff Gabor*

Above: Color key - *by Robert MacKenzie*

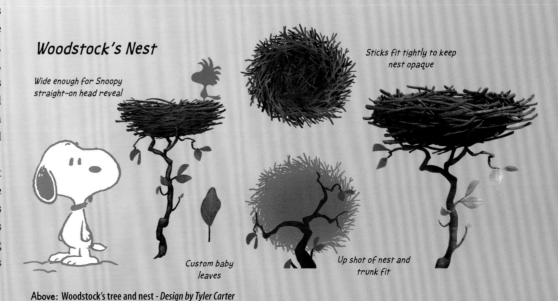

Top: Snoopy's doghouse and toolbox
- *Design by Jon Townley, Model by David Mei and Andre Rodriguez*
Left: *Final Digital Art*

Snoopy's Doghouse

Almost as iconic as Snoopy himself is his signature red doghouse. "Normally, for a protagonist and antagonist, we would use color to play off each other, so we had to balance the red of Snoopy's doghouse against the red of his arch enemy," explains Dunnigan. "The Red Baron's plane is just slightly more muted than Snoopy's doghouse, which is a pure red." Adds lighting supervisor Jeeyun Sung Chisholm, "The red of Snoopy's doghouse is considered one of the hero colors established in the strip, so it was important that no other object had the same color." Because of the sharp, contrasting colors present in Snoopy's Fantasy World, the doghouse can appear a bit darker while still maintaining consistency in design.

An up-close examination of Snoopy's doghouse reveals all the great detail in the bevels, lines and styling that went into the design. "The doghouse was also rigged to be favorably shot in camera," explains Dunnigan. "Like the characters, it needed to feel like the comic, so its perspective could be altered in camera to give the feeling of something we would see in the strips. So not only did Snoopy have a custom rig, his doghouse did, too!"

Woodstock's Nest

Wide enough for Snoopy straight-on head reveal

Sticks fit tightly to keep nest opaque

Custom baby leaves

Up shot of nest and trunk fit

Above: Woodstock's tree and nest - *Design by Tyler Carter*

"*Because we never actually saw the Red Baron in the strip, all our camera angles were cheated so that you can't actually see who is flying the plane.*"

— Rob Cardone, Head of Camera and Staging

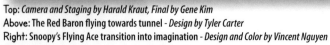

Top: *Camera and Staging by Harald Kraut, Final by Gene Kim*
Above: The Red Baron flying towards tunnel - *Design by Tyler Carter*
Right: Snoopy's Flying Ace transition into imagination - *Design and Color by Vincent Nguyen*

It Was the Greatest Love Story Ever Told...

Above: Aerodrome airplane hangers and barns - *Design by Tyler Carter*

"When the engine backfires on Snoopy, we could have created realistic smoke effects. Instead, we actually animated the little puffs of smoke to match the pen lines in the style that Sparky drew them, and then filled in the shapes with smoke, giving each shape a unique style."
— Steve Martino, Director

Chapter 2 of Snoopy's great novel takes place at an aerodrome and finds the doghouse in need of repairs. Woodstock and his trusty group of Beagle Scouts work diligently on the repairs, but in their haste they forget to install a spark plug, resulting in a backfire that covers Snoopy in soot. Just at that moment, they all spot a plane, a Sopwith Camel. When Snoopy sees its pilot, Fifi, it is love at first sight.

"Alas, he does not make a good first impression," admits Martino. "He's covered in soot and not presentable." In a beautifully lit moment, Fifi hops down from her plane and expertly makes repairs. "Try as he might, Snoopy can't get her attention and just as quickly as she landed, she flies off over the horizon.

Left: Snoopy story beat concepts - *Design by Steve Martino*
Above: *Final Digital Art*

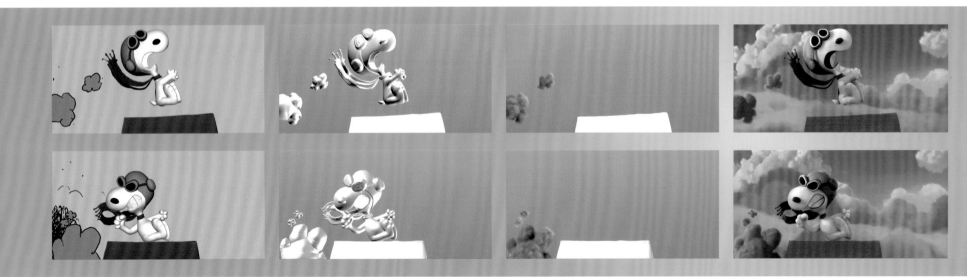

Above: 2D, 3D, FX and materials progression of Snoopy's doghouse backfiring - *Animated by Jeff Gabor, Effects by Ilan Gabai*

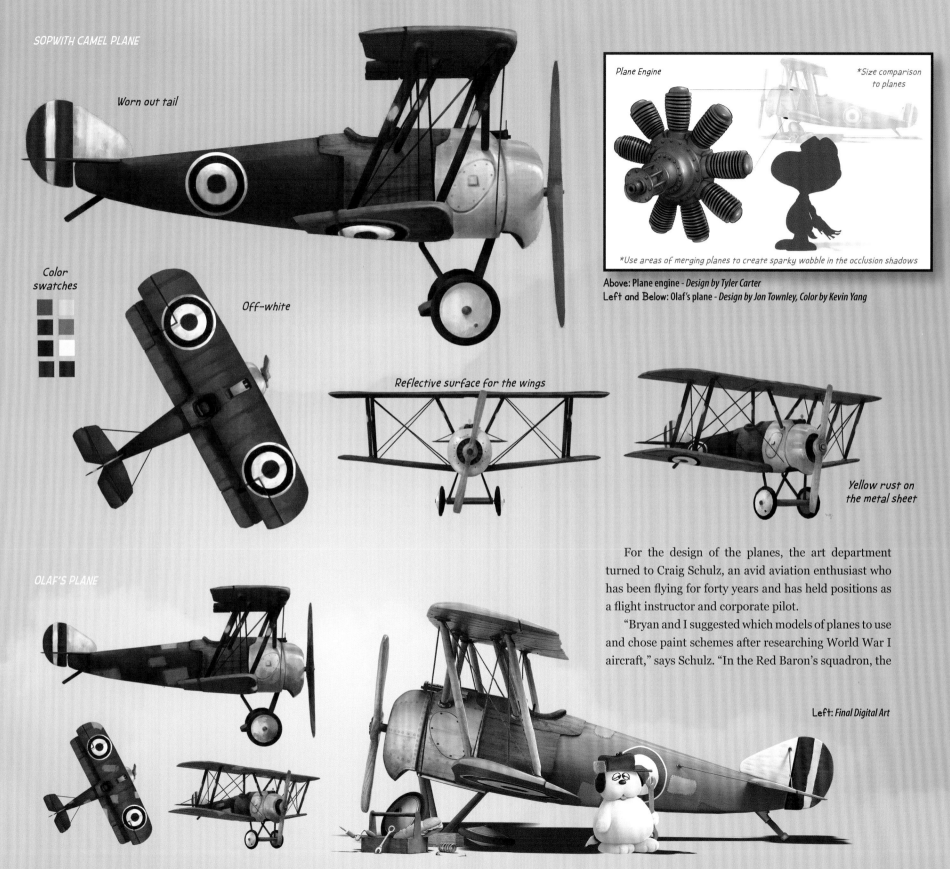

SOPWITH CAMEL PLANE

Worn out tail

Color swatches

Off-white

Reflective surface for the wings

Plane Engine

*Size comparison to planes

*Use areas of merging planes to create sparky wobble in the occlusion shadows

Above: Plane engine - *Design by Tyler Carter*
Left and Below: Olaf's plane - *Design by Jon Townley, Color by Kevin Yang*

Yellow rust on the metal sheet

OLAF'S PLANE

For the design of the planes, the art department turned to Craig Schulz, an avid aviation enthusiast who has been flying for forty years and has held positions as a flight instructor and corporate pilot.

"Bryan and I suggested which models of planes to use and chose paint schemes after researching World War I aircraft," says Schulz. "In the Red Baron's squadron, the

Left: *Final Digital Art*

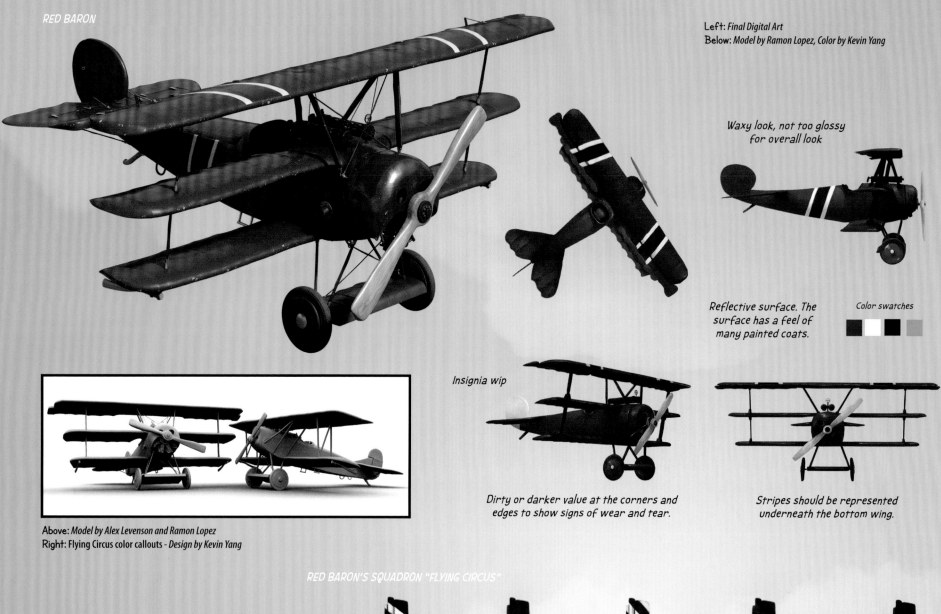

Left: *Final Digital Art*
Below: *Model by Ramon Lopez, Color by Kevin Yang*

Waxy look, not too glossy for overall look

Reflective surface. The surface has a feel of many painted coats.

Color swatches

Insignia wip

Dirty or darker value at the corners and edges to show signs of wear and tear.

Stripes should be represented underneath the bottom wing.

Above: *Model by Alex Levenson and Ramon Lopez*
Right: *Flying Circus color callouts - Design by Kevin Yang*

RED BARON'S SQUADRON "FLYING CIRCUS"

Flying Circus, we used the Albatross for his cohorts and wanted to be sure the audience could recognize his red triplane amidst all the aircraft."

To make Fifi's plane stand out from the other Sopwith Camels, the paint scheme of her plane features a predominately white body so that it would be easily distinguishable.

A.   B.   C.   D.   E.

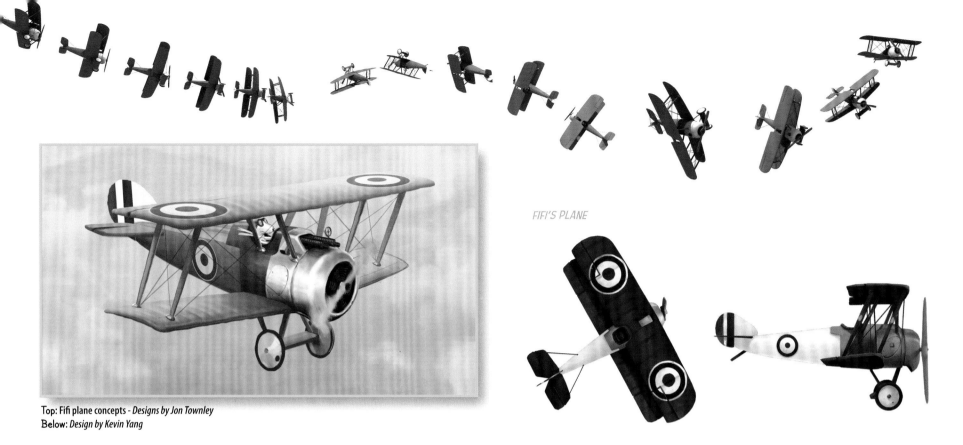

FIFI'S PLANE

Top: Fifi plane concepts - *Designs by Jon Townley*
Below: *Design by Kevin Yang*

He Thought He Lost Her Forever...

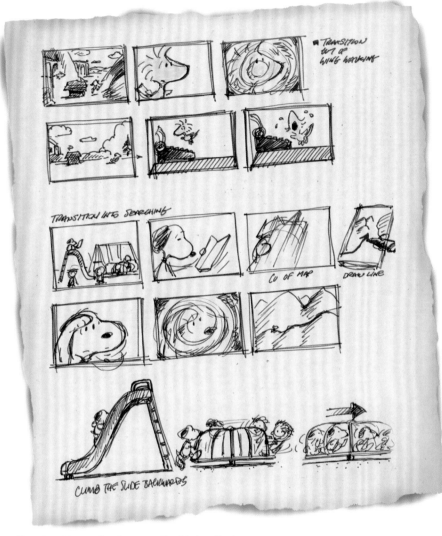

Above: Transition storyboard concepts - *Sketch by Steve Martino*
Above right: Snoopy and Fifi flying - *Color Keys by Ron DeFelice*

The next chapter of Snoopy's imaginary story finds our hero finally meeting the mysterious Fifi, high up in the clouds. The two share a playful interlude, flying their planes, but the moment is too soon interrupted by the appearance of the Red Baron who, to Snoopy's dismay, kidnaps Fifi.

When the time came to animate Fifi, the task was assigned to character animator Lauren Baker, who has a passion for flying. "Becoming a pilot is something I have always been interested in," says Baker. "Animating Fifi flying in her Sopwith Camel alongside the Flying Ace was a great experience for me!"

Above: The Red Baron captures Fifi - *Design by Tyler Carter*

This page: Fifi wingwalking moment painting - *Design by Tom Humber and Vincent Nguyen*

Above: Snoopy and Fifi flying concept art - *Design by Tyler Carter*

Turning to a personal hero of hers, Amelia Earhart, Baker infused Fifi with qualities similar to the aviation pioneer. "She's bold, brave, daring and smart, like Earhart."

To capture the authentic feel of World War I-era planes in the air, the animators researched Sopwith Camels in flight and 1920s-era barnstormers. "For brave and daring ladies in the air," says Baker, "I looked at a lot of material on Amelia Earhart, as well as footage of the modern-day Breitling Wingwalkers, and the late wing-walker Jane Wicker."

Right: Color key - *by Ron DeFelice*

Above: Fifi falling - *Design Layout by Jon Townley, Characters by Dan Seddon, Color by Peter Nguyen*
Left: Snoopy's pocket photo of Fifi - *Final Digital Art*

"While working on the sequences of Fifi piloting her Sopwith Camel, I was extremely inspired to hear the news that Katie Higgins had just become the first female pilot in the history of the Blue Angels."
— Lauren Baker, Character Animator

Left and Above: Fifi and Snoopy flying into the sunset - *Designs by Tyler Carter*

Right: Peanuts, March 29, 1992

Because most of the action in Snoopy's imagination takes place in the wild blue yonder, the filmmakers were able to open up the background by using various shapes and sizes of cloud to give the audience a sense of scale that, in direct contrast to Charlie Brown World, provided for deeper stereo values. Maintaining Schulz's pen line, the art department filled the sky with simplified and organic cloud shapes.

With the freedom they had to expand beyond the more neutral, dialed-down background color palette of the rest of the movie, in Snoopy's Fantasy World the art department was also able to explore multiple color variations in the clouds, using saturated pink and purple hues to help illustrate and emphasize the drama and story.

Right: The Red Baron chasing Snoopy - *Color Key by Vincent Nguyen*

The addition of more saturated colors also enabled the lighting team to broaden their horizons with regard to stylized lighting choices. "With such contrast in the vibrant background colors – that we are not doing in Charlie Brown World – we are able to explore blown-out sunlight and even sun shading with some very extreme back lighting," says lighting supervisor Jeeyun Sung Chisholm.

Right: *Charlie Brown's 'Cyclopedia*, page 450 (volume 10: Featuring People Around the World)

aerodrome   near mountain range   scenic canyons   deep mountain range

Above: Snoopy mountain shape language - *Design by Tyler Carter*
Below: Train bridge and tunnel - *Design by Tyler Carter*

Curse You, Red Baron!

For Jim Kammerud, head of story, the Red Baron chase sequence in Chapter 4 of Snoopy's novel proved not only challenging but also especially creative and fun to storyboard. "In Snoopy's imaginary world, we break out into three dimensions, and really have some fun with our shot selection," explains Kammerud. "What I love about the sequence is the action combined with the mystery, and then all of a sudden this huge spotlight comes out of nowhere and the design becomes simple and graphic once again."

The chase sequence also finds Snoopy on an exhilarating journey over the streets of Paris in an attempt to rescue Fifi from the Red Baron. To recreate the iconic landscape and monuments that populated the streets of Paris circa 1915, specifically the Trocadéro area, the art department researched archives of photos from 1890, shortly after the installation of the Eiffel Tower.

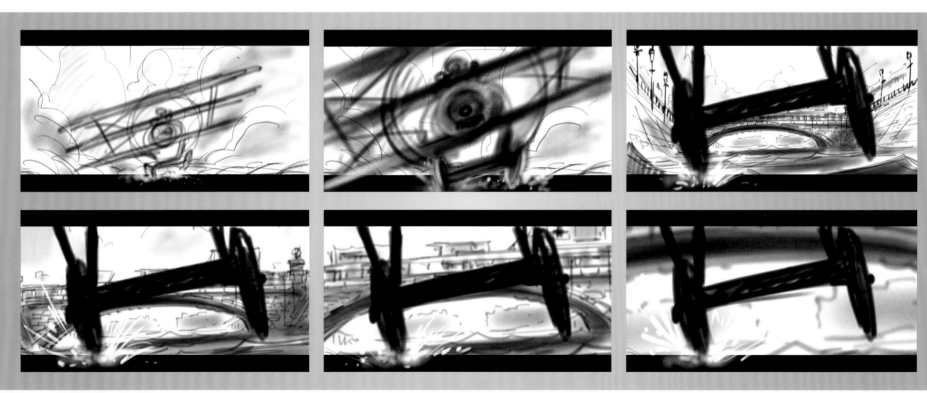

Above: Snoopy pursues the Red Baron over Paris storyboards - *Design by William H. Frake III*

"We wanted to stay true to the era of World War I," explains art director Nash Dunnigan. "By 1930, the Eiffel Tower had undergone slight modifications in the details of the observation deck, as had the civic buildings around the base of the tower, so we wanted to stay as true as possible to the design elements of the era, both for the tower and the Trocadéro area."

"Recreating Paris was a lot of fun," says assembly supervisor Gareth Porter. Working with a team of technical directors, Porter and his team

Above: Snoopy Flying Ace model progression - *Animated by Tab Burton*

Above: Snoopy chasing the Red Baron over Paris - *Final Digital Art*

collaborated with Blue Sky research and development to produce a propagation tool that would enable them to generate new versions of every building by adding different details, such as chimneys, facades, roofing and other slight variations, to the twenty basic buildings created by the modeling team. Although Porter and his team could have used real GPS data to recreate the city streets, they opted to base placement on an authentic map of 1915 Paris. "In the end, we generated nearly 100,000 buildings and covered four square miles of roads," says Porter.

"The Snoopy fantasy sequences of the World War I Flying Ace chasing the Red Baron over Paris are stunning and a great use of 3D technology. The attention to detail is spectacular."

— **Paul Feig,** Producer

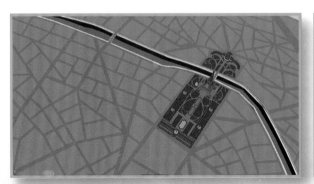

Above: City of Paris - *Assembly by John Kalaigian and Brian Handler*

Above: Eiffel Tower final model - *Design by Sandeep Menon, Model by Alex Levenson and Ramon Lopez*
Right: Snoopy chasing the Red Baron over Paris - *Storyboard by William H. Frake III*

Above: Trocadero building final model - *Design by Sandeep Menon, Model by Alex Levenson and Ramon Lopez*

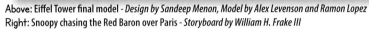

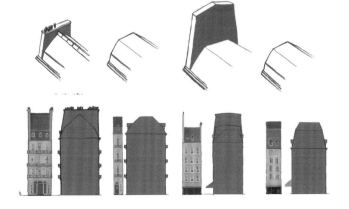

Same design, different lengths

End piece

Above: Paris apartment buildings concept art - *Design by Sandeep Menon*

"In night-time sequences, it was challenging to light Snoopy so that it looked like he belonged in a darker scene where objects are naturally a bit cool in temperature. We had to balance the lighting to make sure he looks as we remember him in daytime sequences and maintain his 'hero/master' look."

— **Jeeyun Sung Chisholm**, Lighting Supervisor

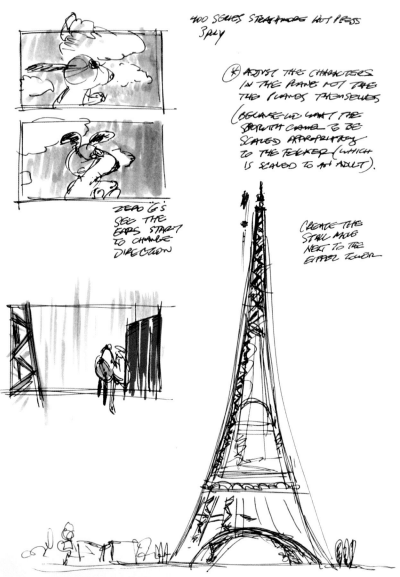

Above: The Red Baron pursues Snoopy Flying Ace - *Design by Vincent Nguyen*
Opposite far left: Snoopy vs. the Red Baron chase flight plan - *Design by Steve Martino*
Opposite: *Final Digital Art*

The Flying Ace Was Lost...

After chasing the Red Baron through the French countryside, Snoopy finds himself stranded. Since the scene takes place at night, the filmmakers wanted to convey a stark contrast to previous landscapes depicted in the story, and particularly Snoopy's Fantasy World. "We needed the landscape to feel desolate, cold and very uninviting," explains art director Nash Dunnigan.

As he seeks shelter, Snoopy spies a possible source of safety in the distance. "In contrast, we needed the chateau on the hill to feel safe and warm; like it was the only refuge Snoopy could find in his travels," Dunnigan continues.

In a nod to Mendelson and Melendez, the artists molded the design of the shimmering full moon after the one seen in the television specials.

When Snoopy snaps back to reality, we find that he is actually standing in front of Schroeder's house.

Above: Color key - *by Tyler Carter*
Opposite: Flying Ace behind enemy lines -
Design and Color by José Manuel Fernández Oli

Above: Color keys - *by Tyler Carter*
Right: Snoopy imagines Peppermint Patty in a French chateau -
Color by Ric Sluiter

Never Give Up!

In the final climactic chapter of Snoopy's novel, the World War I Flying Ace goes head-to-head (or plane-to-plane) with the Red Baron. With Fifi being held captive in a zeppelin air ship, Snoopy is on a rescue mission.

"We knew it had to be the biggest action sequence in the film," explains art director Nash Dunnigan. To help set the right tone, the artists designed large, billowy clouds that suggested skyscrapers to serve as set elements. When juxtaposed against the relatively small sizes of the planes, they conveyed a dramatic sense of scale.

"We wanted to use the scale of the clouds, both in lighting and the shadows that they cast, to add to the drama of the staging as the planes battled around the zeppelin," explains Dunnigan. Ultimately, the passages and contrast of light and dark created by the clouds helped reinforce the intensity of the dogfight.

"We also used the contrast to put emphasis where we wanted to focus the audience's attention," Dunnigan adds.

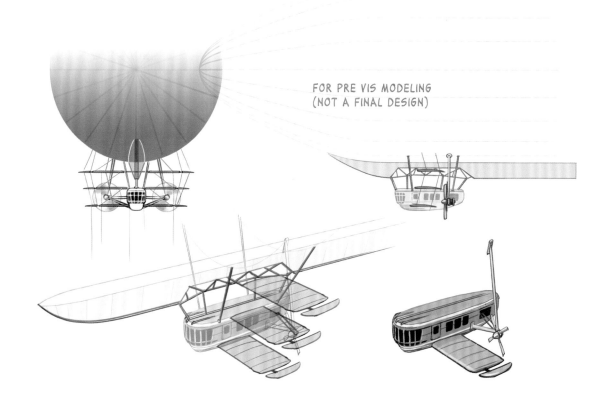

FOR PRE VIS MODELING
(NOT A FINAL DESIGN)

Right: Zeppelin concept art - *Design by Jon Townley*

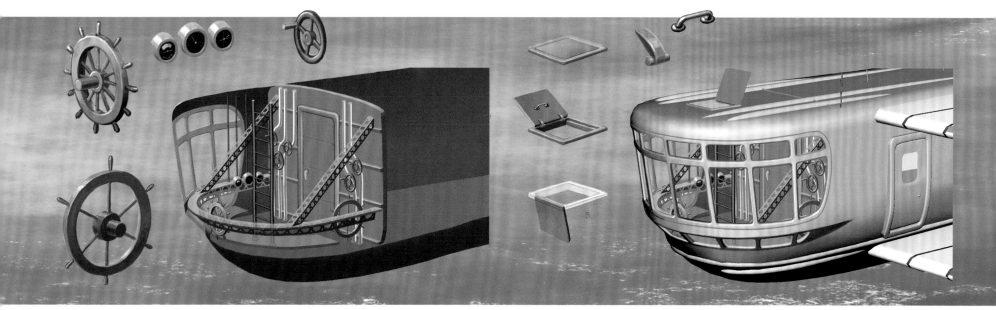

Above: Zeppelin cab design - *Design by Jon Townley, Model by Ramon Lopez*

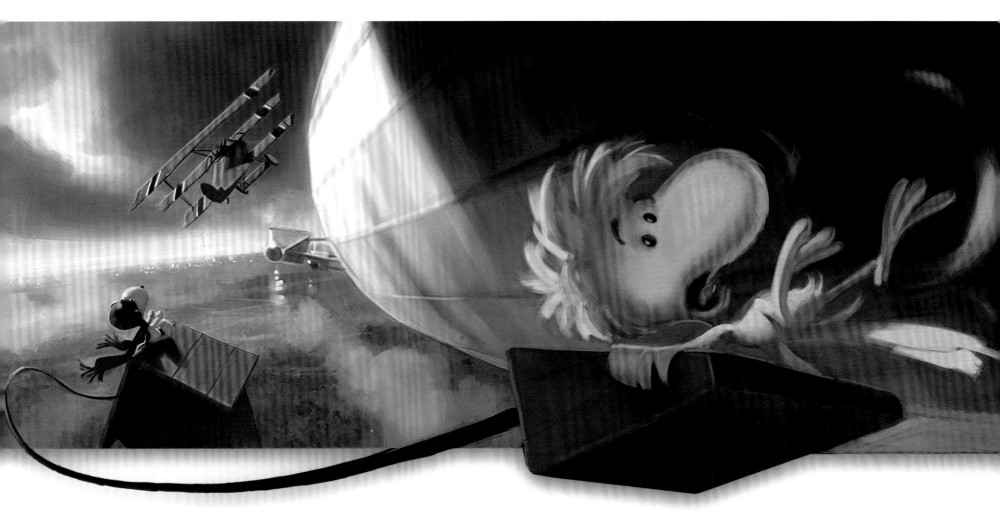

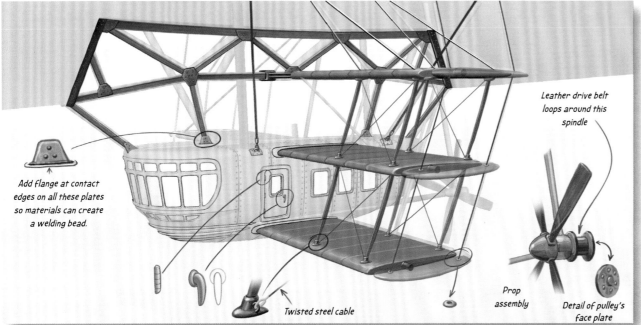

Add flange at contact edges on all these plates so materials can create a welding bead.

Leather drive belt loops around this spindle

Twisted steel cable

Prop assembly

Detail of pulley's face plate

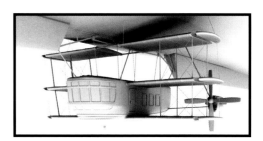

Top: Flying Ace and Woodstock chasing the Red Baron - *Design and Color by José Manuel Fernández Oli*
Left: Zeppelin concept - *Design by Jon Townley*
Above: Zeppelin final model - *Model by Ramon Lopez*

Top: Color key - *by Robert MacKenzie*
Above: Snoopy Flying Ace and Woodstock - *Sketch by Steve Martino*

This page: Snoopy Flying Ace and Woodstock vs. the Red Baron -
Layout by Tom Humber, Painting by Mike Lee

STEREOGRAPHY

Smile, Snoopy! You're In Stereo 3D!

010 KITE STEREO DEPTH SCRIPT

Above: Stereo depth script for skating pond sequence - *Depth Script by Daniel Abramovich*

"I like to relate stereography to scoring for music," says stereoscopic supervisor Daniel Abramovich. "You're using 3D to enhance the emotion for any given sequence and then, when mapping out the pacing, it can often times take on a very moving quality, just like the score of a film can trigger feelings of joy, anger or even anxiety."

Shooting in stereo 3D involves using two cameras that are offset from each other, shooting from two different angles, one from the left and one from the right. The distance between the two cameras will determine how much stereo – or "3D volume" – is in the final shot or frame. The farther apart the cameras are in relation to one another, the more the audience experiences the 3D effect of the scene. Whereas the closer the lenses are to each other, the more their shots will merge into one, lessening the 3D experience.

Abramovich's approach to working in stereo on a movie is to sit down with the director to set standards and figure out what the audience needs to emotionally react to in the 3D. "Everyone's going to perceive it differently, depending on the style of the movie," he says. "Who better than the director to tell you what's going on with the sequence?"

Because sequences are not launched into digital production in story order, a depth script is created to help the stereo team keep track of the overall key beats of the story. In essence, the depth script serves as a stereo continuity script.

"Before a film is launched into digital production, we review the entire film in sequential storyboard order," says Abramovich, explaining how, working with director Steve Martino, he created the depth script. "Taking five key panels from each sequence or major story beat, we create a numerical language, with the number 1 representing minimum stereoscopic volume and 6 representing the maximum stereo volume. We then place arrows and other markers to signal and determine the stereo screen, or where the border is between what recedes behind the screen and what comes forward into the audience space."

"In Charlie Brown World, we are trying to emulate the classic View-Master feel, where everything is behind the screen, almost like a diorama," explains Abramovich. While that may sound simple enough, in fact, certain characters naturally have more 3D than others just because of the way they were modeled. "Because their heads are giant spheres, we had to apply a stereoscopic effect in most of the group shots by isolating any character close to the camera and rendering that character-and-background image with an individual stereoscopic value which was composited towards the end of the pipeline," Abramovich explains.

Managing motion blur, or more accurately the appearance of motion blur through the use of ghost limbs, proved especially challenging for the stereo team.

Lead animator Jeff Gabor, who handled animation sequences for Snoopy, also worked on early animation tests of the iconic "zip lines" that occur in the strips whenever Schulz wanted to indicate a quick or sudden movement of a character or speedy exit from a scene. "We used a 2D software package to create the motion speed lines for those frames," recalls Gabor, "which the stereo department had to take and assign individual [depth script ranking] values to, and place them in the frame to make sure they just don't sit in front of the lens."

In direct contrast to Charlie Brown World, the fantasy sequences in Snoopy's Fantasy World organically called for stereo elements coming off the screen and interacting more with the audience space.

"We did have to reign in Snoopy a bit," notes Abramovich. "Because of the way he is modeled, we discovered that too much stereo 3D made him look off model, almost like a Picasso."

To enhance the fact that the flying sequences take place in Snoopy's imagination, not the real world, the filmmakers took some liberties by miniaturizing the sets and actually animating the distances, which, as Abramovich explains, "Gives the illusion of an accordion effect to the landscape when he's flying around." The end result is a spectacular blend of animation and 3D, giving the sequences a heightened dreamscape feel.

This page: Stereography by Daniel Abramovich - *Final Digital Art*

THE SOUND OF PEANUTS

Happiness is the Sound of Snoopy's Laugh

Above: Writer/producer Craig Schulz and director Steve Martino with actors Mariel Sheets (Sally) and Hadley Miller (Lucy)

Whether it is the heartfelt monologue delivered by Linus in *A Charlie Brown Christmas* or Sally bemoaning the fact that she has been robbed of "tricks or treats" in *It's the Great Pumpkin, Charlie Brown*, the distinct sound of the characters' voices are just as iconic as their looks.

"Those voices are ingrained into my mind," says writer/producer Craig Schulz. Having been through a similar process for the 2011 original direct-to-DVD *Happiness Is a Warm Blanket, Charlie Brown*, Craig Schulz knew first-hand how important it would be to find just the right child actors to bring the Peanuts characters to life. He was also very decisive when it came to reviewing auditions, only needing to hear a portion of a recording to determine whether or not the right voice had been found. "I knew within hearing three words," he recalls.

Working with casting director Christian Kaplan, the filmmakers met with nearly a thousand hopefuls on both the east and west coast, searching for their ensemble. "Sally and Marcie always seem to be the most difficult to cast," says Craig Schulz. "Both are darn near impossible to find."

The most important quality the team looked for was authenticity and believability as a kid. "I didn't want Christian to read or 'audition' the kids, but rather just to have kids talk about their lives, where they went to school, where they're from," recalls Schulz. During the casting process, Kaplan and the filmmakers also recorded lines from the Peanuts specials to gauge each actors' rhythm and cadence to see if they could match their on-screen counterparts.

Working with kids can be a challenge for some, but not Martino. "With all of the kids it's about fun and I said that at the start of every session. There was never a 'wrong' in our sessions, there was only 'trying things,' and laughing when they're good – which I was more prone to do than they were – and allowing time to experiment."

Martino also discovered that his twelve years of coaching youth soccer came in quite handy for wrangling and working with his young cast. "I have always believed in empowering kids, teaching in practice, but letting them own the game," says Martino.

"The great thing about working with kids is that they have extraordinary imaginations, which is huge, given that we are in an empty room, no costumes, no set, no props, only our ability to paint a picture in our minds of the scene we are playing."

After an exhaustive search, Martino found his Charlie Brown in Noah Schnapp, a ten-year-old from Scarsdale, New York. "Noah has a great voice for Charlie Brown, but also has a similar temperament," says Martino. "When we recorded him, it allowed us to rely on his natural tendencies and it really felt like Charlie Brown."

Casting the voice of Linus, however, gave Martino nightmares. Literally. "Linus was my favorite voice from the original Peanuts specials and was the voice I was most worried about casting," recalls Martino. "Linus had this wonderful natural lisp. It was never overdone, but felt so 'real.' I had nightmares about trying to recreate that and having it come off as fake and strange." Fortunately for Martino, his nightmares ended when he discovered his Linus in eleven-year-old Alex Garfin from New York. "In our story, Linus is that steady, supportive friend for Charlie Brown," says Martino, "and like Noah, Alex also has a temperament that feels like Linus."

In a case of life imitating art, young Alex provided a calming presence on set during recording sessions with Martino. "No matter what was going on with me during production, when I would walk into the studio with Alex, I just felt better," recalls Martino. "He had a wonderful attitude, an ability to laugh at himself and to make you feel like the work was fun."

And in a case of life not imitating art, ten-year-old Huntington Beach, California native Hadley Miller is nowhere near her on-screen crabby, bossy counterpart, Lucy. "Hadley has this sweet, well-mannered personality and my initial concern was whether or not she could play the bold, brash side of Lucy's characters," says the director. But all concerns were alleviated when Miller stepped into the recording booth. "She knocked

NOAH JOHNSTON
AS
SCHROEDER

NOAH SCHNAPP
AS
CHARLIE BROWN

HADLEY MILLER
AS
LUCY

ANASTASIA BREDIKHINA
AS
PATTY

WILLIAM WUNSCH
AS
SHERMY

MADISYN SHIPMAN
AS
VIOLET

MAR MAR
AS
FRANKLIN

REBECCA BLOOM
AS
MARCIE

AJ TECCE
AS
PIGPEN

FRANCESCA CAPALDI
AS
LITTLE RED HAIRED GIRL

VENUS SCHULTHEIS
AS
PEPPERMINT PATTY

MARIEL SHEETS
AS
SALLY

ALEX GARFIN
AS
LINUS

Top: Director Steve Martino with actor Noah Schnapp, the voice of Charlie Brown
Above: Hadley Miller, voice of Lucy
Below, left to right: Rebecca Bloom, voice of Marcie; Marleik "Mar Mar" Walker, voice of Franklin; Mariel Sheets, voice of Sally

me over with her big, bold delivery," says Martino. "She really understood Lucy. I said, 'Wow, that was amazing,' and then out of character, back to being Hadley, she said in the sweetest, most polite voice, 'Thank you.' She was perfect."

Producer Michael Travers echoes Martino's sentiments regarding the young actress. "We didn't actually meet Hadley in person until after we had cast her and heard her voice, which was just spot-on," he recalls. "Then we met her and she was this effusively gracious and sweet kid!"

Although she may not have as many lines as Lucy or Peppermint Patty, the presence of the Little Red-Haired Girl in the film is an undeniable force. "It was important that her voice have a sincere quality and to have some degree of sweetness," says Martino. He found his Little Red-Haired girl in ten-year-old Francesca Capaldi.

"I was so taken by Francesca's personality," recalls the director, "that she seemed like someone Charlie Brown would love to know."

Writer/producer Craig Schulz was especially pleased with how the cast shaped up. Early on in the recording process, he attended a voice session of Mariel Sheets, the young actress who portrays Sally Brown. Sheets had no idea who Schulz was at the time, and during a break, Schulz recalls how she rattled off lines from the Christmas and Halloween specials, beat for beat, with perfect pacing. "She was phenomenal," he recalls. And rounding out the cast is Micah Revelli, the great-grandson of Charles Schulz (and grandson of Amy Schulz), who represents the fourth generation of the Schulz family to be credited on the film. Micah voices the character of Little Kid, who appears in a few scenes throughout the film.

Although the voices of the kids had been cast, there was one more crucial voice to cast: Snoopy. Schulz knew there was only one person who could bring to life the world's most beloved beagle, and that person is none other than the legendary Bill Melendez. "It was really important for us to use Bill's voice, so I approached his studio and secured the majority of the recordings he had made over the years," says Schulz.

In addition to obtaining Melendez's performance recordings of Snoopy, the filmmakers also secured his recordings of Woodstock.

For the final sound mix of the film, director Steve Martino turned to two-time Academy Award-winner and long-time Blue Sky collaborator Randy Thom, and his

team at Skywalker Sound, who had already worked with both Martino and Travers on multiple productions. With more than twenty credits on animated films alone, including the two *Rio* films, Thom is no stranger to the challenges of animation and designing a world of sound from scratch. "It's a wonderful thing to work in a variety of styles," says Thom. "What I particularly enjoyed about this film is that directive and challenge set by Steve [Martino] that we stay true to the original sound of the Peanuts TV specials, which I found especially intriguing.

"Even though we're using contemporary equipment, we're employing special techniques to antique them," continues Thom, "incorporating characteristic sounds you'd recognize from the specials." One of those techniques is using ribbon microphones similar to the ones used by Bill Melendez and Lee Mendelson.

Entrusted with the recordings of Melendez, Thom took special care incorporating them into the film. "We studied his voice and the recordings he made at the time," explains Thom. "[Melendez] would record himself doing just hums and purrs and whistles and modulate his voice up and down, and then he would later alter the pitch higher so that it was a funny little creature. The trick of course is to invent a language that is expressive emotionally but isn't comprised of words, just sounds that are halfway between an animal sound and human vocalization, and to be funny when appropriate and of course affectionate when appropriate."

The filmmakers also turned to one of the world's top new musical artists, Billboard Music Award-winning and Grammy-nominated Meghan Trainor, to pen an original song for the film.

"Meghan has written a wonderful song titled 'Better When You're Dancin'" that expresses Charlie Brown's optimistic attitude as he works with Snoopy to become a better dancer," says Martino. "She is such an amazing singer-songwriter and a shining example of the thematic heart of our story."

According to Martino, Trainor met with the team at Blue Sky, then seemingly overnight captured the essence of the film in song. Continues the director, "Musically, Meghan had me from her very first rough demo; my foot was tapping and I had a huge smile on my face as I could see this moment in the movie being lifted by her unique talents."

Above: Schroeder plays his piano, while Charlie Brown plays the dog in Peanuts, March 28, 1999

Play It Again, Schroeder!

No movie about Charlie Brown, Snoopy, Linus, Lucy and the rest of the gang would be complete without the memorable music of Vince Guaraldi and his iconic theme 'Linus and Lucy,' which debuted in *A Charlie Brown Christmas*.

Arguably one of the most recognizable themes ever written, the filmmakers always knew it would be used in the movie, the question was where and when? Ultimately, it was decided to use the music cue early on. "It felt appropriate to have Vince Guaraldi's music in the opening sequence," explains director Steve Martino, "in order to provide the audience with a memorable touchstone early on in the film."

Working with the film's composer, Christophe Beck, jazz legend David Benoit recorded new tracks of Vince Guaraldi's classic 'Linus and Lucy' for the film. No stranger to Snoopy, Charlie Brown and the gang, Benoit has been a staple of the Peanuts world since 1989, composing, arranging and performing on numerous specials. Rounding out the music of the film is New Orleans' very own Troy Andrews, aka "Trombone Shorty," who will "perform" the vocals – or more precisely, the "wah-wah-wah, wah, wah-wah" sounds used to represent the adults' speech in the film.

Left: Francesca Capaldi, voice of the Little Red-Haired Girl

FROM STORY TO SCREEN
The Making of Sequence 010_KITE

"When it came to the opening of the film, the very first thing that I wanted to do and see as a fan – and for anyone else watching – was to convey a familiar feeling that 'It's going to be OK,'" says Martino. "And more importantly, we wanted to pay homage to Sparky's legacy. So the movie starts off with his pen line and that pen line fills in with the look of our movie."

That pen line clearly set the tone for the entire film. "As the opening shot in the film, it defines much of the visual language that we were still developing at that time," explains CG supervisor Rob Cavaleri. "The 2D animated lines are representative of the comic strip, so we had to seamlessly transition between hand-drawn animated snowflakes and 3D snowflakes that continue forward in the scene."

Above: Color key - *by Vincent Nguyen*
Opposite: Storyboard - *by Chris Siemasko, Bryan Cox, Jeff Call and Jim Kammerud*

Story / Layout

The story opens with the Peanuts gang finding out that school has been cancelled because of snow. It's every kid's dream come true during the winter: a "snow day!"

One by one, we are introduced to the kids as they are getting ready to go outside, all building up to the reveal of our hero, Charlie Brown. "It's like watching the rock star go from his dressing room, walking through the halls, tracking from behind with people cheering, building the anticipation, until he steps out in the arena and the camera cuts to the front for the reveal," says producer Paul Feig.

All the kids quickly gather their hockey gear and head down to the pond. All the kids, that is, except for Charlie Brown. It's winter and the Kite-Eating Tree is without any leaves, giving Charlie Brown the confidence that today might actually be the day his kite takes flight.

"In the opening sequence, we wanted to show that Charlie Brown is extremely persistent and that he never gives up. If he can't get his kite to fly when it's warm, he is going to try in winter, when the Kite-Eating Tree is asleep. We also wanted to show how this affects his relationships with his friends, who either find it charming and admirable, or irritating and delusional."

— **Jim Kammerud**, Head of Story

Above: Ice pond set concept - *Design by Jon Townley*

Color Concept / Assembly

Since this was one of the earliest sequences launched into the production pipeline, the design and assembly teams were still working on their understanding of the overall environment and how all the elements would work together once placed.

"The pond was at the edge of a forest, so initially we wanted to have a background wall of trees that blended together, a mass of trees that wasn't distracting, so we set about dressing the set in that manner," recalls assembly supervisor Gareth Porter.

However, Martino and art director Nash Dunnigan thought the environment looked too crowded and complex juxtaposed against very simple characters and asked the assembly team to do a simplification pass of all the assets (trees, shrubs, etc). "We reduced the number of branches and the materials [surfaces] were simplified so that the bark on the trees looked more like Sparky's pen line," says Porter. His team also revised the set decoration, using simple assets in the foreground and much fewer assets overall, taking out many of the trees and shrubs altogether, leaving only the iconic elements from the strip.

"The strips were smart and dialogue based, balanced with physical comedy. As a kid, I think one of my favorite moments was when Charlie Brown's kite entangled the kids in one giant tree."

— **Paul Feig**, Producer

Below: Skating pond set dressing - *Assembly by Antelmo Villareal*

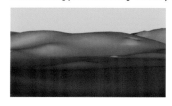

Above: *Final Digital Art*
Right: Ice pond set occlusion renders - *Model by Eryn Katz*

simplified   complex

Above: Maple tree - *Design by Jon Townley*
Right: Maple tree bark materials -
Materials by Brent LeBlanc and William Liu

simplified
materials

original
materials

Animation / Rigging

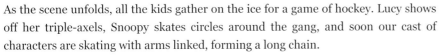

As the scene unfolds, all the kids gather on the ice for a game of hockey. Lucy shows off her triple-axels, Snoopy skates circles around the gang, and soon our cast of characters are skating with arms linked, forming a long chain.

"We wanted to have a level of realism of cutting into the edge of the ice when they skated," says supervising animator Nick Bruno. But animating on twos (12 frames per second) would not have conveyed the fluid movements one would expect to see when watching someone skate. As a compromise, the artists animated the scene using a combination of ones (24 frames per second) and twos.

"All the kids' body poses were animated on twos, while their path of movement on the ice through the physical space was animated on ones," explains animation supervisor Scott Carroll. "Imagine you're watching a moving robot, on a skateboard," adds Bruno, providing the perfect analogy.

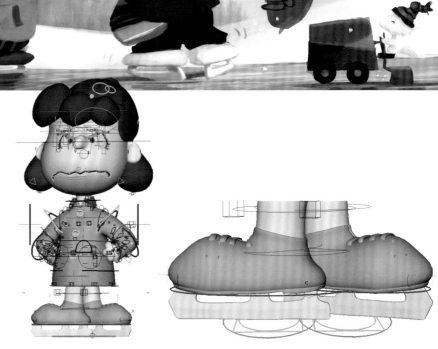

Above: Lucy and her skates - *Model by Krzysztof Fus*

Over the years, Schulz would occasionally illustrate thought bubbles coming from the kite, giving it a personality and point of view. To similarly give the film's kite some character, character development supervisor Sabine Heller's team created a special rig for it.

"String is always a big challenge," says rigging supervisor Justin Leach. "It is basically a long joint-chain which is hard to pose, so rigging the string enabled the animators to give the kite's motion some personality."

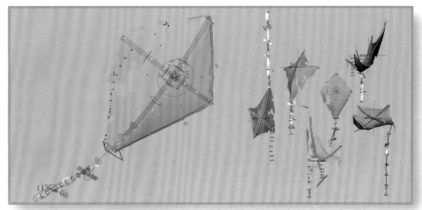

Above: Kite models - *Design by Kevin Yang, Rigging by Jane Chatot*
Left: *Final Digital Art*

Above: Jackets for hero and background cast - *Models by Adam McMahon, Shaun Cusick, Krzysztof Fus and Jonathan Lin, Materials by Svetla Gressak, Travis Price and Heather Brown*

Materials

As with their indoor wardrobe, each of the kids wears a signature color when outside, which, as lead color designer Vincent Nguyen explains, "are basically versions of their iconic summer colors, with the exception of Charlie Brown and Lucy."

Keeping the characters on model required additional rigs for each garment (as with their hero indoor clothes). "[Schulz] drew the kids similarly, if not a little trimmer, when they wore their coats," observes art director Nash Dunnigan.

Just as Schroeder's shirt proved complicated to keep on model, so the materials department faced similar challenges with the specific detailing found in the coats. "Most of the coats have very detailed piping that sets them apart from each other," explains lead materials technical director Nikki Tomaino. "When the characters move, the piping stretches, which altered their iconic shape language."

Adds materials supervisor Brian Hill, "We had to pay particular attention to high-deforming areas around the base of the neck and shoulders." To compensate, the artists would first pose the garments to match the shape of the characters (which depended on how the character was animated) and then the materials team would apply the piping and detail.

Above: Marcie jacket drawover - *Design by Dan Seddon*

Above: *Drawing by BJ Crawford, Color by Vincent Nguyen*

In a humorous moment in the scene, Pigpen is seen trailing the gang while skating in line. When he is yanked out of frame, he leaves behind an echo/outline of himself... in dust.

"Originally our plan was to simulate the poofs, but since it was important to produce shapes and timing in the style of Schulz, the animators created shapes to represent the poofs," recalls effects supervisor Elvira Pinkhas. "We then had to figure out how to translate those shapes in 3D."

Pinkhas turned to senior effects technical director Ilan Gabai (the same artist who created Pigpen's skirt-based volumetric rig for the dust cloud) and effects lead Alen Lai to develop a workflow system that enabled technical director Chris Chapman to fill the poofs with volumes, in correct stereo space. Therefore creating three-dimensional shapes while still maintaining the silhouette from the strip. "The FX

team did a fantastic job of developing a style of animation for Pigpen that had the feel of the comic strip and the TV specials, but worked just perfectly in a Peanuts-style 3D world," praises CG supervisor Rob Cavaleri.

"The bigger pressure for me was the family unit. As a family we strongly decided we would never do a movie, so when I threw out the idea about doing a movie and that I had a story, [then] they all read it... they all liked it, the pressure was to do it and do it well. They've all seen the movie and are thrilled and blown away by what Blue Sky has done."

— Craig Schulz, Writer/Producer

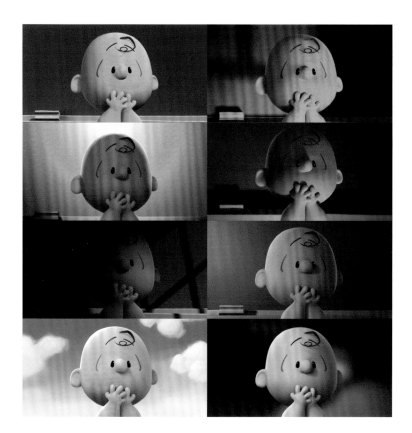

Above: *Final Digital Art*

Lighting

"The opening shot in the movie was deceptively complex," says Cavaleri. "There were many visual and technical challenges that belied the apparent simplicity relative to other scenes in the movie." For lighting supervisor Jeeyun Sung Chisholm, it was crucial to closely monitor balancing the light refracting off the ice and snow and onto the kids' faces. "This is the sequence where we first reveal and introduce our hero, Charlie Brown. With the obvious contrasts due to the subdued background and refracting light, we made sure he was warmly lit."

Left: Time of day lighting tests - *Final Digital Art*
Below: *Final Digital Art*

Author Dedication

For my very own Peanuts gang: Katie, Allison, Kyle, Kiera, and Sophie.

Above: *Blue Sky team photo, courtesy of Travis Price*
Opposite: *Final Digital Art*

Author Acknowledgements

The pages of this book are truly a testament to the brilliant and talented artists at Blue Sky Studios. I simply cannot say "thank you" enough to director Steve Martino, producers Craig Schulz, Mike Travers, Paul Feig, art director Nash Dunnigan, and all the artists quoted throughout this book for their passion and dedication to the film and book.

To Jean Schulz and everyone at the Charles M. Schulz Museum and Charles M. Schulz Creative Associates, especially Karen Johnson and Paige Braddock, thank you for a peek behind the curtain and into the world of Peanuts. It has been nothing short of extraordinary.

At Twentieth Century Fox Animation, a heartfelt thanks to Vanessa Morrison for trusting me with this project, along with Melanie Bartlett, Andrea Miloro, Michael Musgrave, Carlee Weinbaum, Kathryn Laing, and of course, a special shout-out to the company's resident Snoopy, the indomitable Ralph Millero for his tireless efforts and passion for this project.

At Blue Sky Studios, Jennifer Birmingham, Nicole Scaramuzzo for their amazing work in wrangling all the artwork for this project; Chloe Esposito, Jonathan Smith for working me into their production schedules; and Brian Keane, their fearless leader.

Thanks of course to the gang at Peanuts Worldwide – Leigh Ann Brodsky, Craig Herman, Kim Towner, Melissa Menta; Lauren Levine, thanks for the intro.

A special thank you to Kristin Chenoweth for her tireless support of all things Peanuts.

To Titan Publishing's amazing editor and resident Literacy Ace, Jo Boylett, thank you so much for this opportunity, and Alison Hau and Tim Scrivens for a brilliant job on the creative.

And finally... to Charles M. Schulz, without whom none of this would have been possible.

"I'M A BORN CARTOONIST. WHY DO MUSICIANS COMPOSE SYMPHONIES AND POETS WRITE POEMS? THEY DO IT BECAUSE LIFE WOULDN'T HAVE ANY MEANING FOR THEM IF THEY DIDN'T. THAT'S WHY I DRAW CARTOONS. IT'S MY LIFE."

– Charles M. Schulz

About the Author

JERRY SCHMITZ
@JerSchmitz

Despite the fact that Jerry Schmitz grew up with a beagle named Snoopy and a German/Australian shepherd mix named Schroeder, he did not realize he was a "collector" until his mid-thirties, when one Christmas it dawned on him that he needed a second tree to accommodate all of his Peanuts ornaments. In his spare time, when he's not on eBay scouring for 1958 vintage Hungerford vinyl figures of Schroeder and Linus to complete his set, or re-tweeting Woodstock, he keeps busy in the film business as a marketing, publicity and production consultant. He is the author of *The Art of Shrek Forever After* and *Surf's Up: The Art and Making of a True Story, by Cody Maverick*. He will forever be in awe of Sparky.

Bibliography

BOOKS

Carlin, John, and Paul Karasik, Brian Walker. *Masters of American Comics*, New Haven, CT, Yale University Press, 2005

Mendelson, Lee, and Bill Melendez. *A Charlie Brown Christmas: The Making of a Tradition*, New York, Random House, 1979

Schulz, Charles M. *Celebrating Peanuts: 60 Years*, Andrews McMeel Publishing, 2009

Schulz, Charles M. *It Was a Dark and Stormy Night, Snoopy*, New York, Holt, Rinehart and Winston, 1971

Schulz, Charles M. *Peanuts: A Golden Celebration*, New York, HarperCollins, 1999.

Schulz, Charles M. *Peanuts Jubilee: My Life and Art with Charlie Brown and Others*, New York, Holt, Rinehart and Winston, 1975

Solomon, Charles, *The Art and Making of Peanuts Animation: Celebrating Fifty Years of Television Specials*, San Francisco, Chronicle Books, 2012

ARTICLES

Johnston, David Cay. "Connie Boucher, 72, a Pioneer In Licensing Cartoon Characters," *The New York Times* (December 27, 1995)

Melendez, Bill. "Working With Sparky," *Animation World Network* (July 1, 2000)

Schwarz, Alan. "The Nation: Peanuts and Crackerjack; a 50-Year Streak in a Game of Failure," *The New York Times* (December 19, 1999)

Sito, Tom. "Bill Littlejohn: Off We Go... Taking Our Pencils Yonder...," *Animation World Network* (August 24, 2007)

ONLINE

limelightagency.com / Tom Everhart / biography

Schulzmuseum.org / Charles M. Schulz Museum

PEANUTS: THE ART AND MAKING OF THE MOVIE

ISBN: 9781783293247

Limited Edition ISBN: 9781785651199

Published by

Titan Books

A division of Titan Publishing Group Ltd

144 Southwark St

London

SE1 0UP

www.titanbook.com

First edition: October 2015

10 9 8 7 6 5 4 3 2 1

Photo on page 170 courtesy of Mariel Sheets.

Photos on page 172 by Kevin Estrada and Brian Friedman.

Photo of Mr. Schmitz by Shandon Youngclaus.

Titan Books would like to thank the following people, all of who were instrumental in making this book happen: Craig Herman at Peanuts Worldwide; Vanessa Morrison, Ralph Millero, and Melanie Bartlett at Twentieth Century Fox Animation; Jennifer Birmingham, Nicole Scaramuzzo, Angela Macias, Mia Lalanne, Steve Martino, BJ Crawford, Nash Dunnigan, Tyler Carter, and everyone at Blue Sky Studios; Karen Johnson, Cesar Gallegos, and Jennifer Pickens at the Charles M. Schulz Museum; and the Schulz family.

Did you enjoy this book? We love to hear from our readers. Please e-mail us at: readerfeedback@titanemail.com or write to Reader Feedback at the above address.

To receive advance information, news, competitions, and exclusive offers online, please sign up for the Titan newsletter on our website: **www.titanbooks.com**

Front endpapers: Peanuts, August 7, 1983
Back endpapers: Peanuts, April 6, 1997